Earthwise

Environmental crafts and activities with young children

For Jonathan, Joshua and Ava, my children,
and for all children

Earthwise

Environmental crafts and activities
with young children

Carol Petrash

Floris Books

Illustrations by Donald Cook

First published in 1992 as *Earthways* by
Gryphon House Inc., Beltsville, MD
This UK version, edited by Mary Charrington,
published in 1993 by Floris Books, Edinburgh
Sixth printing 2010

British Library CIP Data available

ISBN 978-086315-158-3

Printed in Great Britain
by Bell & Bain Ltd., Glasgow

Mixed Sources
Product group from well-managed
forests and other controlled sources
www.fsc.org   Cert no. TT-COC-002769
© 1996 Forest Stewardship Council

FSC

Contents

2 Winter

3 Spring

4 Summer

Introduction

The environmental problems that confront us today are as varied as they are severe. Some of these — global warming, the depletion of the ozone layer, the destruction of the rain-forests — are on so vast a scale that they seem remote and insurmountable. But over the last twenty years environmental awareness has steadily increased, too. In the Rio Earth Summit of 1992, we see the first tentative steps towards global political agreement on protecting the Earth and its natural life. Clearly the very future of our planet will depend on the degree to which all our children, the world over, are made environmentally aware and respectful of the Earth, and sensitive to a higher quality of Nature.

The task is huge, yet we can all play our part by taking a close look at our own personal or family way of life. Children are naturally suited for this challenge. They come into life with a sense that the world is good and beautiful. Our example as adults, our interactions with them as parents or teachers, and the ways in which we bring children into contact with Nature can either enhance these intuitions or else destroy them. When children find love and respect in the world around them, they will have love and respect to give. Our task as the parents and educators of young children is not to make them frightened of environmental dangers but rather to provide them with opportunities to experience what Rachel Carson called "the sense of wonder." Out of this wonder can grow a real feeling of protective kinship with the Earth.

Through playing creatively with the elements of earth, air, water and (carefully supervized) fire, as well as through nature crafts, experiencing "real" toys which stimulate the imagination, and through the rhythmic celebration of the seasons, we can instil knowledge and with it reverence and respect towards the Earth and the life of Nature. This childhood experience can then mature into adult recognition that the Earth is not a possession or commodity that humankind has a right to exploit, but rather a precious gift which it is our duty to protect.

We do our children a service whenever we turn their attention to natural things — stones, grasses and flowers, trees and animals — or find creative and attractive ways to bring Nature into our homes and classrooms, or go out with them to discover. All children should have the opportunity to delight in the simple sound of a bird's song, the shape of a stone, the texture of a tree's bark, the smell of a flower or of freshly turned earth. Developing a close relationship with Nature in these ways promotes not only the health of our children but the health of the planet as well. Contact with Nature will bring simplicity back into the lives of both children and adults: the simplicity of doing things at Nature's pace, of working through and with Nature's rhythms.

In addition, we must find gentle ways of showing the children the importance of good practices such as recycling and composting, and above all, not being wasteful in our daily habits. For young children, learning by example is preferable, and more effective than any number of heavy-handed lectures and explanations which leave a residue of fear and guilt. Environmental awareness will come naturally to children when it is integrated early on into the classroom and home as a way of life.

SETTING UP AN "EARTH-FRIENDLY" HOME OR CLASSROOM

We have all grown up with the notion that more is better; that if something breaks, we replace it with something new; that there is an endless supply of whatever we need. These ideas are no longer viable, and we need to bring up our children with more environmentally aware habits and attitudes.

How can we be more Earth-friendly? Start by using fewer and fewer items that are thrown away, such as paper napkins, paper towels, plastic cling-film and plastic cutlery. Start using small pottery cups instead of disposable paper cups. Mark each child's name on the bottom of his or her cup, so that the children always use the same cup. They can wash their own cups and let them air dry. You may be able to find a local potter who would make a set of small cups or mugs for children.

Another idea is to make small fabric place mats (approximately 15 cm x 20 cm) for the children to use. Gradually (with the help of other teachers, parents and friends, charity shops and jumble sales) you can accumulate a good set of children's bowls, spoons, forks and knives. Children learn the routine of setting the table with the fabric place mats for meals. Just make sure there are the correct number of chairs at each table, and ask the children to put out the place mats and cups, or whatever is needed. (This is excellent practice in learning how objects correspond — for example, one knife, fork, spoon, bowl, cup and place mat for each person.)

If your kitchen area permits it, set up a dish-washing station near the sink with two tubs — one with hot soapy water and a dish mop, the other with clear, warm water for rinsing — and a drying rack or a draining board. When the children are excused from the table, they wash their dishes before going for their rest. Once this becomes a habit — and it is an excellent one — they become very good at it and actually need little supervision. However, children of three years old, or younger, may need help when washing dishes.

Wash the place mats weekly as part of your usual washing day. Use two wash tubs again — one with soapy water and one with rinsing water — and a good old-fashioned scrubbing board (still available in some hardware shops) and kitchen soap, the type of hard soap that doesn't get mushy in water. Set the tubs on two thick bath towels to catch some of the water, but also just accept that it is water play day. Begin by wetting the mats, rubbing them on the bar of soap (it rests conveniently on the top edge of the scrubbing board) and "scrub-a-dub-dubbing" them up and down on the scrub board. Then put them into the rinsing water, wring them out and hang them up to dry. Use an indoor drying rack or place them in a basket to hang outdoors on a clothes line later. The children love to help with the washing, and, of course, you can always "volunteer" those who seem to need some "watery work" to focus or calm their energy. This is also a good time for washing doll's clothes or bedding or other cloths or linens that need it. Once the washing is done, take out cups, ladles and egg beaters for water play.

BREAKING THE "THROWAWAY HABIT"

Here are more suggestions for breaking the "throwaway habit."

Oil or vinyl cloth

Use oil cloth (nowadays often made of vinyl and known simply as PVC) instead of newspapers for covering tables during messy activities. It can be wiped clean and endlessly re-used. Remember that it is not thick enough to prevent scratching a table surface so you may want to put a protective cloth underneath. PVC is available in some fabric or hardware shops and usually in large department stores.

Children's cloth aprons

These aprons can be washed and used over and over again for cooking, baking, painting, and so on. They can be easily made from thick kitchen or hand towels by following the following pattern:

Step 3 Run a piece of thin rope or cord up through one pocket, over the top and down through the other pocket.

Step 4 Make big knots in the ends of the rope or cord so it will not easily slip back through the pockets.

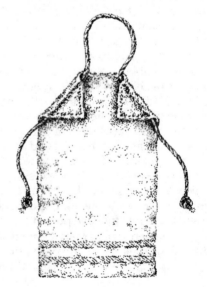

Step 1 Fold over the top corners.
Step 2 Sew down to make two flaps, or pockets.

Step 5 The cord slips over the head and ties behind the back to secure the apron.

Work folders

Make a folder for each child by folding a large sheet of sugar paper or card (approximately 30 x 40 cm) in half. Keep the children's drawings, paintings and so on, in these folders. When you have collected a large amount, make the children's work into a book, rather than letting it remain in dribs and drabs. This helps children learn, from an early age, that their work is valued and should be treated accordingly. Encourage the children to use both sides of the paper when drawing.

Recycling

Most communities across the country are beginning to see the need for and the good sense inherent in recycling. Have special bins in your classroom (the type with built-in lids work well) in which to place items such as glass, plastic, metal and aluminium to be recycled. Remove the lids and rinse and air dry containers before placing them in the bins. When the bins are full, take them to bottle banks, can banks, paper collection centres and so on. Enlist other parents' or teachers' help; perhaps children and families can take turns bringing materials for recycling.

Some local communities now have paper recycling schemes. Local shops may be able to participate by acting as collection points, and in return they could be supplied with recycled paper bags for use in the shops.

If recycling becomes a habit for you, children will imitate it. They don't need lectures about landfills filling up. Just tell them in a matter-of-fact way that it's good for the Earth when we save these things, so that they can be used again and made into something new!

See the Appendix for details of organizations giving information and advice on recycling.

Composting

Composting kitchen and garden waste is a wonderful way to get excellent soil for gardening and planting projects. Generally speaking, if something grew out of the Earth, it can be composted. This includes vegetable and fruit scraps, grass clippings, weeds, leftover scraps of bread from meals, and so on. Do not include meats, fats or packaging of any kind.

A compost heap can be as simple as it sounds — a pile of things you want to compost standing in a quiet corner of the garden or playground. Or, you can be sophisticated and buy a recycled plastic or cedar composter from a garden centre or hardware shop. These have the advantages of being very tidy and animal proof. They do cost some money; however, there are a number of reasonably priced ones on the market. You can find compost bins at garden centres or hardware shops (see Appendix).

To make your own compost heap, dig a shallow hole about 15 cm deep and the size you want the heap to be; put coarse materials in the bottom, such as small branches, sticks and weeds to allow air to circulate upwards, and then add the compost material as necessary. Keep a shovel nearby to chop up the things you add so that they will decompose more quickly. Cover the new additions with a thin layer of soil from the 15 cm that you excavated. You can also use grass clippings and sawdust. Mulching products and organic manure (see Appendix) are excellent for covering a compost heap. When your heap is well covered it is less likely to be disturbed by animals.

Again, composting can get much more sophisticated and detailed than this. This is not the definitive work on composting; it is meant to show you that you *can* do it. It is possible to just "let it rot." If you are in an urban area, one of the more "purpose-built" composters may be necessary to deter unwanted rodent visitors. It would be a bit of an investment, but one that would last for years. And if you tell the garden centre or supplier who you are and what you are trying to do, they may respond helpfully.

It is amazing to see the children's attitude towards previously "yucky" stuff — potato peelings, leftover bread — change when it just, as "a matter of fact," goes into the compost bucket to be taken later to the compost heap to go back to the Earth. Children intuitively respond to the "rightness" of these things when they see that the adults around them know and care.

Repairing toys

When classroom toys and equipment break, don't throw them away! Have a place, such as a big basket, to collect things that are broken and need repair. Once every couple of weeks or so, take out tools, glue, toothpicks, and so on. Bring the basket out, sit down and mend what was broken. You really will be able to mend most things, and, again, the children will love to help. It gives them a wonderful sense of well-being to see things made whole again, and it helps them to develop a conscience about throwing things away. The children I taught used to believe that I could mend anything. They would even tell their parents that they could take broken items for repair — a wonderfully positive attitude!

ENVIRONMENTAL ISSUES

Toxicity

Whether a product is toxic when used is important to consider for supplies and materials that will be used with young children. But, another aspect to consider is whether there are long term effects caused by the production or disposal of the product. Does its production or disposal cause the pollution of water, air or land? Is it made from petroleum or other resources that are non-renewable? Is the packaging environmentally sound? How will it be disposed of?

It is important that we answer these questions and confront these issues. We need to apply this knowledge in our daily lives and in our homes and classrooms. The children learn from what we do, whether we want them to or not. If we display an attitude of conscious caring for the Earth, and act responsibly in choosing the most Earth-friendly products available, this will have a lasting influence on the children.

Fortunately, the task of researching the background of supplies and materials is being made easier as more people become concerned about the effects of these products on their own health and the health of the Earth. Many books are now available to help us make sound choices from the myriad of products available.

The other thing to remember is that once we get used to choosing and using more Earth-friendly products, it will just become second nature to do it. The key here is a change in perspective and attitude.

Packaging

Another factor to consider when buying supplies and materials of all kinds is the packaging. Work toward the idea that less is more in this realm. That is, buy things in large quantities so less packaging is required for each product. Single items or individual glue jars and so on, should be avoided. If you need paste or glue for each child, buy a large jar and put some on saucers or in bowls for individual use.

If you can find products that are packaged in other than plastic containers, choose those whenever possible. Plastics are made from petroleum products and last forever. Just take a walk on any stretch of beach and take note of all the plastics that wash ashore. They don't break down, and even though some plastics can now be recycled, that is not the case for all types. Although it is very difficult to find certain kinds of items in recyclable containers, just keep looking and asking for alternatives and, in the meantime, make the most environmentally sound choices you can. And buy as little packaging as possible. If you can find an alternative to non-recyclable plastic, use it! For example, use grease-proof paper as a wrapping for sandwiches instead of cling-film or plastic bags (the inner bags of cereal packets also make excellent sandwich bags).

Time

Another issue to consider when purchasing things for use with children is the time required to find and to use an Earth-friendly product. It may take longer, but the time is well spent. Consider it an investment in the future of both the children and the Earth. Good habits, once established, go a long way toward making our lives more environmentally aware.

Money

This is a tricky one! The environmentally sound alternatives may be more costly initially. But if you were to consider the hidden costs — damage to the environment and health problems resulting from pollution, the picture changes. For example, buying cloth napkins or place mats might cost more initially than paper napkins, but you'll have them for a year or more. When they are no longer good enough for table use, they can be used to mop up spills, and so on. That will save a few trees in time. Another example is crayons made of beeswax — a renewable resource — as opposed to standard crayons made from petroleum products. The beeswax crayons cost more initially, but they don't break and are more pleasant to use. If you clean them, they can last for years, depending on use (see Appendix).

A good guideline is not to make choices based solely on money. Make the choice by considering the question from an environmental perspective as well. If you need to buy fewer crayons because they cost more, so be it. You can teach the children to share and to really appreciate and care for the things they have.

In brief, if something can only be used once and thrown away, try not to buy it at all and consider responsible alternatives.

Now that we have some guidelines for choosing supplies and materials, let's take a look at the different types.

Cleaning and household supplies

This is another area where less can be more. Plain soap, vinegar, baking soda and borax can accomplish most of your cleaning needs — even combatting germs. Using simple, non-toxic cleaning products is not only better for the environment, it's much less expensive. A good range of commercial Earth-friendly cleaning products is now available in most supermarkets (see Appendix).

Schools are often faced with insect or rodent problems of various kinds and again, there are non-toxic alternatives. If you are working in a school, you could request that these alternatives are explored for large scale use, and that your classroom be spared any applications of toxic materials. Be sure to keep things clean and dry and to remove sources of food and drink, so that any small creatures are encouraged to look elsewhere. If you have a problem with mice, consider a live trap which lets you relocate the mouse to a more suitable habitat.

Art and craft materials

The key is to keep using, as far as possible, materials — paints, pastes, glue, markers — that are water-based, as they are generally less toxic or even non-toxic. Read labels and ask questions.

Crayons made from beeswax are available in blocks as well as sticks. The block crayons are very nice for pre-school children, as they are easier to hold and they don't break.

Use recycled paper for drawing and crafts whenever possible, and encourage the children to use both sides of their paper. Look for natural paints, often standard tempera, watercolours and finger paints are formulated with various chemicals, including formaldehyde. Natural watercolours are available in a wide array of colours. I used jars of red, blue and yellow that seemed to last forever. Mix them in glass jars with tight fitting lids and store the remaining paint in the jars for re-use. Mix just a bit of the colour (start with a teaspoon) in a half-litre of water and test it for strength. Remember that watercolours are not supposed to be as opaque as tempera paints. If you buy just the three primary colours — red, yellow and blue — the children can mix any other colours they need right on their paper. This can be a very exciting exploration. If you dampen the watercolour painting paper first by dipping it in a tray of water, the colours are more fluid on the paper and the painting experience is delightful.

There are books that provide detailed lists of alternative art supplies. In general, stay away from professional artists' materials. They are often more toxic. If something has a strong smell, the kind of smell that children can't resist, like marker pens and solvents, it is best to look further.

Details of suppliers of art and craft materials are given in the Appendix.

Food and drink

If we want to be more conscious about the things we have around the children, it follows that we would also want to be aware of what goes into them. Make an effort to obtain the most healthy, wholesome snacks and meals possible. Ideally, this means food that is free of chemical additives and preservatives and that is organically or biodynamically grown. Food that is produced in this way is not only better for the children but also better for the Earth because the farming methods used to produce this food are life sustaining. Organic whole foods may be more expensive, but it would be better to have less of something that is really good and can be consumed conservatively, than to have lots of mediocre food that can actually encourage wastefulness. A good rule is that everyone sits at the table and has, at least, a taste or tiny portion. This encourages the children to stretch their taste buds and contributes to the social atmosphere.

Look for child-sized cutting boards and knives (round-ended knives do work and aren't dangerous), so the children can be involved in the preparation of their food. In this way, you can avoid packaged snack foods which are neither environmentally sound nor always healthy for children to eat.

Organically grown food is becoming more readily available, but you may need to track down a source in your area. Make use of your own garden as well, then you can be totally sure of the freshness and the quality of what you consume. (See Appendix for more details on the availability of organic foods.)

Good food, just like good crayons and good paper, should be thoroughly enjoyed and appreciated. Take the time to foster appreciation and gratitude and habits of careful, conservative use in the children while they are young, and it will bear fruit for years to come.

Make meal time special by setting the table (a small vase of flowers adds a nice touch), settling everyone and setting the mood with a short grace or verse of thanksgiving before you eat, such as the following:

> Earth who gave to us this food,
> Sun who made it ripe and good;
> Dear Earth, dear Sun, by you we live.
> To you our loving thanks we give.

TOYS FROM NATURE

Many of the "educational" toys that fill our homes and classrooms are not only costly but thwart the innate creativity of the child. They are designed to accomplish a process carefully thought out by adults and, therefore, allow for little creative input by children. The best toys are the simplest — those that allow the "player" to use his or her individual imagination, and can be used for many different purposes. For example, a basket of small stones can go into building a wall or a road; they can be stirred into a "soup"; they can be counted as money for the shopkeeper; they can be tokens for a ride on an imaginary train or bus: they can be used for whatever the play situation demands.

Besides the creative possibilities and the economic advantages they offer, toys from nature have the added benefit of being "real," that is, they come from the Earth and not from a factory. They are durable, beautiful and interesting in their shape, form and colour. They are pleasing to see and to handle. This offers quite a contrast to Day-Glo, non-biodegradable plastic toys. The "un-earthly" look of many commercial "animal toys," to take only one example, makes a sad statement about attitudes to the natural world.

Building blocks and props

Gradually use more natural materials in your home or classroom. With the children, begin to gather stones, shells, pine-cones, anything that nature offers. Carefully wash and dry the stones, and sort other objects into appropriately sized baskets.

Bring in a few small branches and logs. Set up a woodworking bench, and let the children help you saw them into slices. These make excellent building blocks, and offer a wide variety of building possibilities, sometimes more challenging and more interesting

than building with the more uniform square and rectangular blocks. However, you may need to use sandpaper to smooth down some of the rougher surfaces to protect against splinters. You can also drill small holes in the sides of some of these smaller "blocks" and insert small round sticks into the holes to make fences.

Someone who knows how to use a chain saw could cut a whole basketful of these natural blocks for you. Make them varying lengths and try to cut them fairly flat, although those with slanted cuts offer interesting possibilities too. Wax and polish the blocks if you like, or just use them as they are. Over time they will develop a lovely patina.

Introduce these natural building materials by telling a story with them. Once you have gathered a number of different things, sit down and set the scene. Spread a large cloth — preferably earth or grass coloured — on the floor or build on the carpet if you have one. Show the children a little river (a long blue cloth), its banks lined with stones. The river flows down out of the mountain (a pile of stones) and runs past a forest (a stand of pine-cones) and a farm (a house built of wood pieces, surrounded by a stick fence and, perhaps, some small wooden animals). The river flows all the way to the beach (white or sandy coloured cloth and shells) and the sea (a big blue cloth). Here comes a little girl or boy (small wooden figure) travelling down the river to the sea. Just imagine (the children will!) all the adventures she or he will have along the way.

Little stories like this help the children to get started using these new materials. If they are not used to having open-ended materials for play or if their imaginative capacities have not been developed, it may take a bit longer to unlock this hidden potential. This, unfortunately, may be the case if children have been accustomed to sitting passively in front of the television. But all children are born with the capacity for creative, free play. We need only be supportive facilitators.

Tree stumps

Another gift from nature that is very versatile and useful in the home or classroom is tree stumps. These are a little harder to come by, but even in cities, old or dying trees are cut down or trimmed, and it just takes a little effort to contact the people responsible for this kind of work. I have fond memories of trying to roll a tree stump one metre in diameter (heavy!!) up a ramp and into the school van. A parent had told the school about work being done on trees in her neighbourhood. Two of us managed, some-how, to get quite a few stumps. Pre-school teachers can be very persistent! The stumps, varying in size from 30 cm to 1 metre in diameter and from 8 cm to 60 cm in height, became a focal point of our classroom play situations and were the impetus for much real and earnest work.

We spent lots of time removing the loose bark from some of the stumps. We used rasps and files and sandpaper to smooth the rough edges. The larger pieces of bark went into a basket. They served a variety of purposes — as roofs for little buildings, as boats with leaf sails and even as loaves of bread in the "bakery."

One day we used an auger — a large hand-operated drill — and with much effort and lots of turn taking (with the children), managed to drill a large hole in the centre of the largest oak stump. Into this we placed a 120 cm long pole — the kind sometimes used for broom handles. A cup hook screwed into the top of the pole enabled us to attach a pulley so we could raise and lower a flag. A smaller pole lashed on at the bottom allowed us to attach a sail, and many happy days were spent aboard this "ship."

Other stumps became walls, seats on buses or trains, stools and chairs in a house — any number of useful things! What an activity for exercising motor skills on a large scale, moving the stumps around the class-room! The smallest stumps (8-10 cm thick) were often placed on top of other stumps and used as steering wheels! And other times we tied small "oxygen tank" logs on the children's backs so they could be deep-sea divers. As you can see, children are very creative and resourceful when given mate-rials which encourage the use of their im-aginative capacities.

Filling your home or classroom with toys from nature offers children endless creative possibilities for play. It also surrounds them with the warmth and beauty of the natural world, nourishes their senses and fosters, in a subtle yet solid way, their appreciation of all the many gifts that the Earth offers us.

CREATING AN OUTDOOR PLAY AREA

As with using natural materials for toys and playthings indoors, many of the materials that can transform an outdoor area into a "more natural" play area are free for the asking and will work just as well in a back garden or a school yard as they will in an open field. They just require a little time and effort to track them down and install them where you want them.

Stumps and logs

As with indoors, stumps and logs — even larger than we could use indoors — make wonderful additions to the play area. Logs, whole or split lengthwise and placed in interesting arrangements, are wonderful for climbing and walking on and encourage children's creative play in many ways. We had a wonderful old log with a twisted branch at one end that was sometimes a dragon, other times a boat, a train or a tree house. A log, especially a split one, placed over a depression in the earth (dig one with the children if there are none) makes a wonderful bridge. You could line the "river" under it with stones.

Shorter logs, 60 cm to 1 metre in length, can be used to transform the sand area. Children love to play in sand and little sandpits are really too small to play in. It's good to be able to accommodate the vigorous play of lots of children with a large sand area. Lay the logs end to end in a large circular form. Introduce a standing stump every now and then that can be used as a table or "oven." The sand is then dumped into the centre and fills the form. Some of it will squeeze out between the logs, but most of it stays put. The logs are great seats, and the whole construction is great for balancing and walking. A sand pile this size allows for all kinds of play, from real digging with child-sized garden shovels to small building projects and cake bakeries.

Smaller logs or branches (approximately 10-15 cm in diameter) can be used to build a nice climbing structure. The thicker pieces are sunk into the ground upright to provide good support. Then shorter and longer pieces are bolted onto the uprights at various heights and angles to connect them into a climbing structure. Very interesting to look at, and fun to play on!

Wood chips

This natural material can transform a tarmac yard into a forest underfoot! Often wood chips are available free from utility companies who trim around wires and poles. We have often obtained them by just speaking to the operator of the chipping equipment when we saw them working in our area. They were happy to have a place to dump a load or two. We literally carpeted over a tarmac playground with wood chips that are now over one metre thick. We marked out paths with thin logs and filled in everywhere else. Once we built up the base, we had several wood chip "mountains" which we left intact and which provided lots of possibilities for running and jumping and a change of view from our otherwise flat play area.

The garden and the compost heap

The garden was an important part of our outdoor play area, and the compost heap stood in a quiet corner. We discuss setting up these areas in more detail elsewhere (see *Outdoor gardening with young children,* page 25, and *Composting,* page 13) but it is important to mention here what an integral part these played in our outdoor time each day.

For many adults surrounded by children, time outdoors is a time to let go and relax. While these are important, outdoor time is also a good time for work for both adults and children. After a chance to chat a bit, we'd take the brooms and sweep the walks, or shovels or rakes and go into the garden to plant or weed. Child-sized wheelbarrows carried our weeding to the compost heap; watering cans were filled and used to give our plants and flowers daily drinks. We also did our harvesting at this time. Since the

garden was so close to the sand pile and play area, supervision of the children was not a problem.

The other thing that was interesting to note was that as the adults worked earnestly, so did the children. Some of them would immediately come to do whatever we were was doing. Having good quality, child-sized equipment available facilitated their work. But it became clear that even those who weren't helping us directly were much more focused and earnest in whatever they were doing when the adults too were involved in real work. Children learn an immense amount from doing what we do. They also learn more than we can imagine from *how* we do what we do.

Landscaping

Once you get your basic outdoor play area organized and naturalized, you can begin to add the landscaping touches that will make it really special. There is growing interest in landscaping with plants that provide food of various kinds from fruits to nuts, and in plantings that will attract birds and other wildlife. These both provide possibilities for bringing the children into closer contact with and, ultimately, developing an appreciation for, the wonders of the natural world.

Many of these plantings can be done in raised beds or boxes and in containers of various kinds, so don't let an urban location stop you from "greening" your outdoor play area. It can be done, and the benefits will surprise and delight you. This is also a good area in which to muster local help and support in raising funds to buy trees and plants. Organizing work days to get the transformation under way can go a long way towards building a sense of community and fostering an understanding of what you are trying to bring to the children.

CREATING A SEASON'S GARDEN

Creating a small season's garden or corner in your home or classroom is one way to bring nature in and celebrate the rhythm of the seasons of the year. Young children thrive on rhythm — not the rigid holding to a timetable but the rhythmic flow of one thing into another. It gives them a sense of security and well-being to know that as it was, it shall be again. For many children today, their connection to nature and the passing of the seasons is one of the few constants in their lives. So it is all the more important to emphasize this connection and provide a space for recognizing and celebrating it.

Where?

Set aside a quiet corner somewhere in your home or classroom that is out of the way yet accessible to the children. It is good to have a small table which can be the focus, but you could also use a shelf of a bookcase or part of a counter top. A large tree stump (about a child's height) would be especially attractive — keep your eyes open for work being done on trees in your neighbourhood and ask.

A small, round table is especially attractive, as the roundness is a more natural shape and suggests the circle of the year.

What?

Once you have decided where the season's garden will be, you can begin to create it. One of the first things to consider is colour and how you will use it to create the appropriate seasonal mood. Think about the different seasons and which colours they suggest to you. This may be very individual and will certainly be related to the part of the world you're living in. In the United Kingdom with four definite seasons, the following are suggested:

Autumn: Warm colours — soft reds, browns, oranges and golden yellows;
Winter: Cool colours — soft greens and blues, browns, white;
Spring: Pastel colours — pinks, pale yellows, spring greens, violets;
Summer: Bright colours — blues, greens, reds, yellows, pinks.

Find or dye small or medium-sized cloths in these various colours and keep them in a special box so you have them when needed. Charity shops and flea markets are good sources for nice old linens, napkins and so on, that you can use. Dyeing is fun to do with the children (see Appendix).

If your season's garden focal point is a table, you may want to cover it with a white or other neutral colour cloth and use smaller, seasonal cloths as colour accents.

Another touch that is attractive to add is a medium blue backdrop cloth to represent the sky. This works especially well if you are setting up your season's garden in a corner. Hang the cloth from a point 60-90 cm above the garden, and drape it gently down and around the edges of the garden, tucking its edges under the seasonal cloths. Light or medium weight cheesecloth (available in most fabric shops or on market stalls) works very nicely for the sky cloth.

In fact, cheesecloth — particularly the medium weight — is a wonderful, fairly inexpensive material to have in the home or classroom for cloths of all kinds, from those you use in the season's garden to play cloths for the children. Get some friends or other parents or teachers together and buy it by the box as that can make it even cheaper.

Now what?

Your season's garden now has a home and a colourful beginning. What else does it need? Remember that this little place is one in which to celebrate the turning of the seasons and the treasures each season brings. Encourage the children to bring seasonal treasures from nature that they find in their gardens or on walks. If you live in a more urban area, be sure to take them to places where they have a chance to gather seed pods, nuts, coloured leaves, special stones, wild flowers and any other gifts from the Earth that they can find. Going back to the same places at different times of the year allows them to experience closely the changes the seasons bring.

Other things that can be part of your season's garden are seasonal produce — also a gift from the Earth — and things that you make from natural materials.

Having a small dish garden within your season's garden is also very attractive. A clay plant saucer, suited to the size of the garden, with some kind of protective surface between it and your cloths or table to protect from dampness, works very well as a place for growing things. Place some small rocks or pebbles in the bottom of the saucer for draining and fill it with soil. Then it's ready to accept whatever you'd like to plant, from bulbs (autumn) to moss (winter) to seeds (spring). You can also add a nice rock or two, a small piece of bark or an interesting branch or piece of driftwood. Individual seasonal suggestions accompany each season's garden section of this book.

Caring for the season's garden means keeping it neat and beautiful. It should not become a junk corner. This will mean sorting through it occasionally, removing some objects when there are too many and organizing the remaining objects so that they are easy to see and appreciate. Water the plants and seeds, put faded flowers in the compost and, generally, just tidy up. Watch for things like dandelions which can suddenly surprise you by opening up and sending their silky contents floating around the room. As always, gently remove any little insects to the outdoors.

Natural objects that you remove can be used elsewhere. Rocks can go into a basket to be used for building (see *Winter,* page 57, for ways to use natural materials indoors). Seed pods and so on can be saved for various projects. Especially attractive or unusual items can be stored for next year's garden.

Encourage the children to come and play by or in the season's garden, exploring its treasures, but a good guideline to follow is that things stay in the garden and don't travel to other areas of the room. The season's garden should be kept and valued as a special place.

You can have a special time each day when new things that have been brought for the garden can be placed there, perhaps with a brief story about how or where they were found. The idea is not to study things scientifically at this point, but to enjoy and, especially, appreciate them.

OUTDOOR GARDENING WITH YOUNG CHILDREN

For children to cultivate the Earth and to have the realization that all the food we eat comes from the Earth as a result of our labours, helps to develop an attitude of stewardship. It really is true, as well, that children are much more likely to eat things that they have grown themselves. Encourage these experiences by taking the time and trouble to garden with your children. More than any other activity, gardening creates a direct relationship with living and growing things and with the pace at which Nature goes.

Picking the spot

Choose the sunniest spot that is available, whether it is a corner of the garden or playground or a small area under a window. If you live in a city and have no green area, you can start a garden in containers or troughs. It is always a good idea to tell close neighbours what you are doing and to remove any difficulties, whether personal or official, from the start.

Try to situate the garden adjacent to your children's play area, so that gardening becomes a natural extension of playtime outdoors.

Remember that a garden also needs a certain amount of protection, not only from animals but also from humans who may try to undo your work or help themselves to your produce. In some town areas, patience, dogged persistence and a sense of humour may be called for.

Preparing the garden

When starting out, remember that you can begin with a small area and get bigger as you go along. Your garden needs to have beds which are not too wide, with paths between. Children should be able to reach to the middle of a bed from a path on either side. In that way, they don't need to walk where the plants are growing. For container gardening, you can use almost anything from half-barrels to window boxes to boards nailed together into a frame.. The important thing is to have sunlight, to enrich your soil, and not to overcrowd the plants.

For preparing the garden, you will need small forks and rakes; well-composted manure and garden mulch (suppliers of organic products are given in the Appendix); perhaps new top soil or sand; buckets or wheelbarrows; hand trowels. Buy good quality tools; even old used ones are better than cheap plastic products which will soon break. Garage or car-boot sales are good sources and auction sales often have garden equipment.

If you have chosen an area that is grassy, the grass must be dug out with a spade or garden fork. Shake off the soil back on to the plot and use the grass in your compost heap or to patch up bald areas elsewhere. If you plan a season ahead, you can thoroughly mulch your plot area with wood chips, leaf mulch or well-composed manure. The mulch will kill the grass and turn it into soil nutrients which can be spaded in the following spring.

Turn over the soil to aerate it and loosen it. Add nutrients (compost, manure or leaf mulch). Eventually you'll be able to use your own compost! If the soil is very heavy with clay, spade in some sand and work the sand in, which will help to break up the clay.

Choosing what to plant

The important thing is for the children to see the produce themselves, so if you are all going away in June or July, make sure you sow varieties which are ready early. Alternatively, you can sow for harvesting in the autumn but then someone will need to tend the garden and water the plants over the summer.

Suggestions for quick-growing vegetables are: spinach, lettuce, radish, early beans and potatoes. Herbs such as mint, camomile, parsley, lavender and thyme also give good results, especially in window boxes. Some of these spread, so don't plant them just anywhere! Flowers such as marigolds, forget-me-nots and pansies give pretty displays and are easy to grow.

Most seeds can be started indoors weeks before you want to plant them out in the garden. Saved egg-boxes make good seed boxes for tiny seeds such as herbs and lettuce; if you start the seed off in half an eggshell, just lift out the shell, gently crush it and place the whole thing in the ground when planting out.

Herbs such as lavender, sage and thyme can be harvested for brewing herbal teas, and hung in bunches to dry for cooking and making herbal sachets.

Caring for the garden

Weeding (a little at a time) and watering, are
daily tasks, depending on the weather.
Weeds will shoot up after rain and a flat
(Dutch) hoe pushed across the ground at
root level is the quickest way to clear them.
Mulching will help to preserve moisture in
the soil during dry periods and will also help
control the weeds. A good watering can with
a fine spray head is useful, and if you can set
up a barrel to catch rainwater off a roof, you
will be providing your garden with the best
water it can get.

1 Autumn

The season's garden in autumn

For more detailed information on setting up a season's garden, see page 23.

Colours: soft reds, browns, oranges and golden yellows.

Objects: seed pods of all kinds; acorns; conkers; nuts; sycamore and ash keys; corn on the cob; autumn flowers; weeds; pressed leaves and autumn produce (apples, pears, blackberries, sweet chestnuts and so on).

Special Additions: Make a Harvest Wreath with the children to hang over or near your season's garden. Start with a straw wreath frame (available at craft shops) and attach sheaves of wheat and pressed leaves to it. Hang apple slices for drying (see *Drying apples*, page 40) and small bunches of washed seedless grapes from the wreath.

Dipping the bunches of grapes in boiling water will hasten the drying process by breaking the skins and sterilizing them against mould, but this isn't required. Hang the wreath up with red ribbon, and add to it as autumn goes along. Don't forget to eat your dried apples and grapes (raisins) for a snack one day.

This wreath can become a permanent part of your season's garden, changing with the seasons. It also represents the circle of the year.

Planting: If you have an actual indoor garden, conservatory or greenhouse, plant small bulbs like crocuses or hyacinths in it. You could have a little autumn planting "ceremony" — tucking the bulbs in the Earth to sleep through the winter.

AUTUMN ACTIVITIES AND CRAFTS

Leaf banners *Age 3+*

Capture a falling leaf and make a beautiful banner which the children can display.

You will need
- small branches (1-2 cm in diameter) cut into 15-20 cm lengths
- work table covered with an oil or vinyl cloth (PVC)
- old toothbrushes
- jar lids
- red, yellow and brown non-toxic tempera paints
- several large well-formed leaves
- natural coloured cotton muslin cut into 20 cm squares (use pinking shears to prevent unravelling)
- tacks or stapler
- string

What to do

1 Write the child's name in the bottom corner on the back of the cloth.

2 Let two or three children work on their banners at one time.

3 Show the children how to place a leaf on the muslin and splatter paint around the edge of the leaf by dipping a toothbrush in paint and scraping it over the edge of a jar lid.

4 Splatter paint all the way around the leaf, lift it up and see the imprint left behind.

5 Attach the banner to the branch with tacks or staples. Tie a piece of string to each end of the branch.

6 Allow to dry and use as is, or repeat the above steps the next day on the other side to make a double-sided banner.

Wheat weaving   *Age 5+*

Plaited wheat straw decorations — often called "corn dollies" — are symbols of good luck and prosperity. They are part of the harvest celebrations of many countries.

These make lovely additions to the season's garden or decorations for the snack table, especially at a harvest celebration. They also make great napkin holders!

You will need
- wheat on the stalk (from craft supply stores, florists or from farmers in your area who grow wheat)
- tub of water
- red wool

What to do

1 Soak the wheat stems (be sure the seed heads are out of the water) in the tub of water for about an hour before you want to use them.

2 Group the children in pairs and give one child in each pair three stalks of wheat. One child holds the seed heads and the other one plaits. Help the children to start plaiting the stems, beginning at the end near the seed heads.

3 Do a simple plait. Chanting the following helps.
> *Put the right one in the middle.*
> *Put the left one in the middle.*

4 Make the plait fairly tight, and plait the entire stem.

5 Curve the plaited end around, overlapping it with the seed heads and tie with a red wool bow.

Play a weaving ring game with the children including the younger ones. Stand in a circle,

holding hands, and chant or sing (just make up a simple tune) the following:
> *Harvest crown, harvest crown*
> *Now we weave a harvest crown*
> *(Mary) weaves, (Joseph) weaves*
> *Now we weave a harvest crown.*

Name two children standing side by side. When the children are named, they cross their arms in front of them and re-make the circle, holding hands with crossed arms. Gradually sing your way around the circle, calling pairs of children to weave until you've "woven" the whole circle. After the last pair sing or chant:
> *Harvest crown, harvest crown*
> *Now we've woven a harvest crown.*

This a very simple little game, but the children never cease to wonder at the weaving of it. The little ones may need help crossing their arms, and make sure they stand close enough together in the circle so that they can reach each other.

Leaf crowns *Age 2+*

This is a nice activity to do while you are outdoors with the children. Sit and make the crowns while they play, offering them to those who ask.

You will need
- lots of recently fallen leaves with stems. Use fairly large, freshly fallen leaves , as very dry, brittle leaves will disintegrate quickly.
- a basket to hold the leaves

What to do

1 Spend some time gathering the leaves you will use. The children will want to help you with the gathering.

2 Sit in a place where you can see the children playing and where they can see what you are doing.

3 Take two leaves and remove the stem of one at its base. Overlap the tip of one leaf and the base of the other and use the stem to attach the two leaves by pushing it down through the place where the two leaves overlap and back up again, like a pin.

4 Continue to attach the leaves to each other in this way. Try the crown on a child's head, and when it is big enough, attach the last leaf to the first in the same way.

5 Continue to make crowns for other children. Encourage the children's imaginative play by addressing them "in character": "Leaf Family," "Prince Autumn," "Queen Autumn," and so on.

6 Make leaf crowns to decorate your home or classroom.

7 Ask the children to join in the activity by bringing you more leaves, removing the stems or, with older children, making their own crowns with assistance if needed.

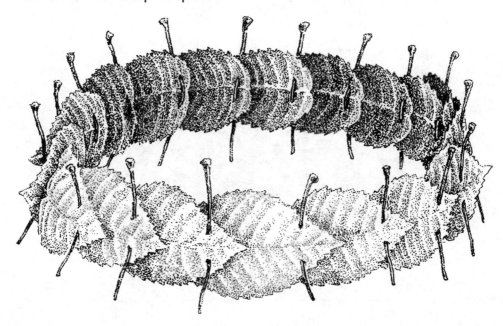

Nature's people   *Age 4+*

These little characters take on their own personalities depending on the materials used and the clothes you add. They are also very handy for "peopling" your season's garden.

You will need
- various kinds of nuts in the shell (acorns, walnuts, beech nuts, conkers and so on)
- pine-cones, nut casings, conker shells, sycamore and ash keys and so on (whatever is available in your area)
- glue (tacky glue is good because it is fast drying — or use white glue or carpenter's glue)
- bits of wool felt for clothing. Try to get felt with a very high wool content if you can as it is sturdier, and nicer to work with (see Appendix).
- scissors
- black felt pen

What to do

1 Select two nuts, pine-cones and so on, and glue one on top of the other to make a head and body. Position them according to the "character" you wish to create. For example, hazelnuts have pointy ends that make a nice face. Some nuts such as conkers have a slightly flat side where a head can be attached. Acorn "tops" make good caps. Some pine-cones have flat bottoms; these make good bodies.

2 Add a scarf, hat, shirt, cloak and so on, by gluing on bits of felt.

3 Use a felt pen to add dots for eyes, but do not draw in all the features. Leave that to the children's imagination.

4 Play with these little people in the sand pit or in little towns or scenes the children create. They add a lovely touch to your season's garden, and they are delightful peeping out of a table's centrepiece.

Lanterns   *Age 3+*

As the days grow shorter, we all need to prepare ourselves for the cold days and long nights of winter. The lantern is a symbol of this: each person carrying his or her own light. Use the lantern at home as a lovely autumn centrepiece or the focus of a special night time lantern walk.

NOTE: As with all activities involving candles, children should never use their lanterns unsupervized, and never leave lanterns burning when you are not nearby.

You will need
- heavy sugar paper, card or heavy white watercolour paper approximately 21 x 30 cm (A4) or 30 x 40 cm. Size is not crucial, so you can experiment a bit.
- crayons or liquid watercolours and paintbrushes
- scissors
- tacky glue, white glue or glue sticks
- stapler
- paper fasteners or thick wire (5 mm)
- warming candles or night lights, sometimes called "tea-lights" (available at grocery, hardware or kitchen shops)
- sellotape
- tissue-paper (optional)

What to do

1 Ask the children to decorate their lantern papers by colouring or painting them. Suns, moons and stars are appropriate decorations, but younger children will just make colour designs. Let the children choose how to colour or paint their lantern.

2 Make a fold all the way across the length of the paper, approximately 8 cm up from the bottom.

3 Cut a fringe of 8 cm wide segments all along the bottom folded section.

4 Cut several small shapes out of the top portion of the lantern. These are the "windows" that the light shines through; they can be circles, random shapes or shapes cut in the sun, stars and moon motif. The sun can be just a circular cutout with snips or coloured "rays." Older children (4+) can cut their own shapes, though they may need help starting the cuts. Small pieces of coloured tissue-paper glued over the windows create a beautiful effect.

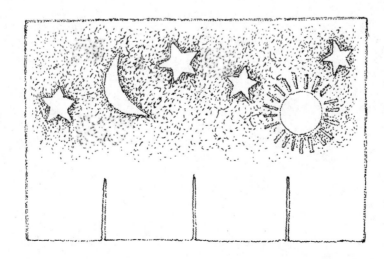

5 Form the lantern paper into a cylinder,
   stapling it at the top and bottom. Fold the
   fringed edges in and overlap them to
   make the lantern's bottom. Put small
   dabs of glue between the fringes to hold
   them together.

6 Add a fairly long handle (30 x 38 cm) of
   either thick wire (5 mm) poked though
   the sides and twisted back up onto itself
   to secure it or 1 cm wide sugar or
   watercolour paper strips attached to
   each side of the lantern with paper
   fasteners.

7 For the light use night lights that come in
   individual metal cups. A loop of sellotape placed in the bottom of the lantern
   holds the candle in place.

mmm mm

Leaf lanterns *Age 3+*

This is a lovely pressed leaf lantern that is more transparent and a bit more fragile than the other style.

You will need
- pressed leaves of various kinds
- wax paper
- scissors
- round lids
- iron and ironing board
- warming candles, or night lights
- white glue
- sugar paper or card strips 2.5 cm wide in autumn colours
- thick wire (5 mm) or 1 cm wide paper strips and paper fasteners
- sellotape

What to do

1 Begin collecting the leaves and saving the round lids two to three weeks ahead of time.

2 Press the leaves by placing them in the pages of a heavy book (telephone books work well) or in a flower press. The children love to help with this. The leaves will be pressed in two to three days. Press enough leaves for all the children.

3 Ask each child to select a lid and cut two sheets of wax paper to fit around the outside of the lid. The lids are the bottoms of the lanterns, the wax paper the cylindrical sides.

4 Each child chooses pressed leaves and arranges them on one sheet of wax paper.

5 Cover the leaves with another piece of wax paper the same size and, using a warm (not hot!) iron, gently but firmly press the wax paper, melting the wax and ironing the leaves between the sheets of paper.

6 Glue a 2.5 cm wide strip of sugar paper (autumn colours: orange, brown, red, gold, yellow, and so on) along the top of the wax paper. This reinforces the top when you attach the handle and gives the lantern a more finished look.

7 Glue the bottom edge of the wax paper to the outside of the box lid. The easiest way to do this is to run a bead of glue all along the outside of the box lid. Then roll the lid along the bottom edge of the wax paper, forming the cylinder as you roll. You may also add a finishing strip of sugar paper or card along this bottom edge.

8 Put several dabs of glue along the overlapping edges of the wax paper sides to close the cylinder.

9 Attach a 30 x 38 cm handle using 5 mm wire poked through the sides and twisted back up and around itself several times to secure it, or 1 cm wide strips of sugar paper or card attached with paper fasteners.

10 Place a loop of sellotape in the bottom of the lantern and add a night light.

"Dandelion seed clocks" *Age 2+*

Watch for these full dandelion seed heads from late spring through to autumn. Dandelions grow wild and are often found along the roadside.

You will need
- "dandelion clocks" (if possible one for each child)

What to do

1 Take the children outside on a breezy day and help them find good, full dandelion seed heads.

2 Either encourage the children to hold the dandelions high above their heads and run with them so that the silky seeds can fly free. Or with slightly older children play the "dandelion clocks" game: Ask the children the question "What's the time?" They answer by blowing seeds from their dandelion heads and chanting "One o'clock" and so on each blow. The final answer is the one they chant when they blow the last seeds from the dandelion head. Obviously, different children will have different final answers but this doesn't matter; you can see which one is nearest to the actual time.

3 Back at home or in the classroom you can act out the following rhyme with the children:

In a dandelion cradle all close and warm,
(Place cupped hands together)
Little seeds are hiding safe and warm. (Keep hands closed)
Open wide the cradle now, hold it high.
(Open cupped hands, raise them above your head)
Come along wind, help them fly. (Sway open hands in the air)

APPLES

Drying apples *Age 4+*

Drying apples is a good way to store autumn's harvest and save it up for winter. If you have access to an apple tree or trees all the better. Then the children can do the picking as well.

You will need
- 10-12 whole apples
- sink or large bowl
- towels
- basket or bowl
- sharp knife for the adult
- small knives for children (normal table knives will work but look for smaller round-ended ones, or buy paring knives and "pre-dull" them)
- vegetable peelers
- small cutting boards
- small bowl
- aprons for everyone
- large needles
- thread

What to do

1 Fill the sink or large bowl with water and put the apples in it.

2 Let the children rinse them, dry them and place them in a basket.

3 Bring the apples to the table and peel them with the children, using the vegetable peelers (the apples dry more effectively with the skins removed).

4 With the sharp knife, slice the peeled apples horizontally into 1 cm thick slices. Surprise! Notice the star in the centre of the apple. Show the children how to cut around the centre to remove the star and pips. You will end up with apple slices with a round hole in the centre. (NOTE: Save the apple pips in a small bowl.)

5 Using pieces of thread about as long as your arm, thread large needles with doubled thread, knotting the thread about 8 cm from the end.

6 "Sew" through the first apple slice by going through the hole and then back through the doubled thread. This will secure the apple by knotting it to the end of the thread.

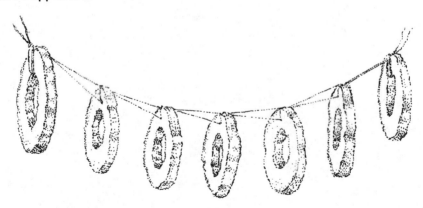

7 After securing the first apple slice, ask the children to continue the "sewing." They sew right through the apple pulp, slide the slice down toward the last apple slice and then sew back up through the doubled thread. Leave a bit of space between each slice so that air can circulate between them.

8 Each thread is finished when no more apple slices will fit on. Knot the last slice in place as you did the first.

9 Hang the strings of apple horizontally in the room to dry. Possible places are from plant hangers; from the harvest wreath if you have one; from hooks attached to the ceiling; from a pole or broomstick attached to the ceiling at each end so that it hangs horizontally. This will accommodate lots of strings of drying apples.

NOTE: It is important that the apple slices air dry slowly, so they should not be hung in strong direct sunlight. Also each slice should be separated from the next so that air can circulate around it. If you have lots of slices that are close together, they can get mouldy before they are able to dry out. If the slices are slipping together on the string, you may need to adjust them or knot them in place.

ALTERNATIVE METHOD: If you want to avoid the stringing process, you can hang the apples horizontally by threading them onto a thin stick, cane, or length of pole. Hang the stick by supporting each end. You can fit lots of apples slices on a single pole, and even the youngest children can easily slip the apple slices onto it.

SEED SAVING: For all the apple activities, save the pips that you remove from the apples, string them with needle and thread and dry them. They are actually quite beautiful and make lovely chains and decorations for the harvest table or your autumn season's garden. Be aware that apple pips can be poisonous if ingested in large amounts. While you are saving them, keep the jar out of the reach of younger children.

Cutting apple shapes   *Age 2+*

This is fun to do at meal time or if someone has brought an apple for a snack. The children will watch in amazement and be delighted by the results.

You will need
- apples
- sharp knife

What to do

1 Crowns: Make sure the apple is washed. Using a sharp knife, cut apple crowns by cutting the following pattern all the way around the middle of the apple:

Be sure to cut well into the centre of the apple but not all the way through. Hold the top and bottom of the apple. Give a twist and pull the halves apart! Surprise! Two crowns. The children will have fun putting them together and taking them apart again.

2 Puzzles: Cut puzzles by cutting this pattern all the way around the apple. Continue as with crowns.

3 Stars: Cut the apple horizontally, just above or below the centre, to find the three-dimensional star. Another way to find this is to eat the apple (or pear) whole. When you begin to get close to the core, nibble gingerly so that you get as much pulp as possible off the little core, or seed house, without actually disturbing it. Let this seed house dry and you have a three-dimensional five-pointed star. This, again, provides great excitement for the children if you bring it to them in an enthusiastic way. It's also a great way to encourage them to eat their whole apple!

4 Mushrooms: Make a horizontal cut all the
  way around the apple, just below the
  centre. Then make four straight cuts
  from the bottom of the apple in to the
  horizontal cut, as if you were cutting a
  square around the core. Take off these
  straight cut pieces, turn the apple the
  right side up and you have a mushroom.

Making apple
sauce   *Age 3+*

Another way to store autumn's harvest is to make apple sauce for meals or snacks.

You will need
- sharp knife for the adult
- round-ended knives (short handled ones if possible) for the children
- cutting boards
- large pot
- stove or hot plate
- food mill
- large bowl
- spoon
- cinnamon or nutmeg
- honey, brown sugar, or syrup (optional)

What to do

1 Wash and dry the apples. If they are not organically grown, you may want to peel them to remove as much of the pesticide residue as possible.

2 Using a sharp knife, cut the apples in quarters, slice out the cores and put them in the compost bucket.

3 Give the quartered, cored pieces to the children to chop and slice on their own cutting boards. The nice thing about this step is that it doesn't really matter how they cut them. Round-ended knives work fine for this. (NOTE: Before handling food, always make sure that the children wash their hands thoroughly.)

4 Place the big pot in the middle of the table and put all the pieces into the pot.

5 After you have chopped all the apples, put the pot on the stove to cook on medium to low heat and add about 1 cm of water. If the stove close by, cook the apples while the children are doing other activities, and let the wonderful aroma fill the air. Just stir it occasionally to make sure it doesn't burn. If your access to a stove is limited, other cooking alternatives include cooking the apples in a crock pot or cooking them at another time. (NOTE: If you use a hot plate, take the necessary safety precautions and tell the children clearly that they must not get too close.)

6 When the apples have cooked down and are quite mushy, let them cool and then bring the pot, a large bowl and the food mill to the table. Attach the mill to the edge of the bowl. Put several large spoonfuls of apples into the mill, and let the children take turns milling the apples. Every so often you will need to stop and clean the skins out of the bottom of the mill. These are great for compost if the children don't nibble them all up.

7 After you have turned all the apples into sauce, season with a bit of cinnamon and/or let the children grate a bit of nutmeg into the sauce. Occasionally, if you used only tart apples, you may want to add a little sweetener (honey, brown sugar, or syrup).

8 Enjoy the apple sauce!

Baking whole apples *Age 3+*

Baking apples whole or turning them into cake are two other delicious ways to bring autumn's harvest into your home or classroom.

You will need
- large baking pan (pyrex works well)
- large bowl
- mixing spoon
- large apples (preferably organic so the skins can be eaten)
- apple corers
- goodies for stuffing: chopped walnuts, raisins, date pieces, currants, and so on
- cinnamon or nutmeg
- sweeteners: honey, brown sugar, or syrup
- milk or cream (optional)
- spoons and bowls

What to do

1 Wash and dry the apples.

2 Mix the stuffing ingredients with a bit of cinnamon and/or fresh grated nutmeg and some sweetener.

3 Show the children how to use the corers to core the apples.

4 After putting the cores in the compost bucket, stuff each apple with the stuffing mixture. Children love to do this, and even the youngest can help.

5 Place the apples in a baking dish and add about 1 cm of water.

6 Bake the apples in an oven at 180°C, 350°F, Gas Mark 4 for about an hour. A delicious snack or dessert!

7 Serve in bowls with a bit of milk or cream if you like.

Baking apple cake

Age 3+

This tasty cake is easy to make and uses the
fruits of autumn's harvest.

You will need
- 100 g melted butter or margarine or oil,
  plus extra for greasing the cake tin
- 200 ml syrup or honey (or some of each)
- 1 teaspoon vanilla
- 200 g whole wheat flour
- 1½ teaspoon baking powder
- 1 teaspoon salt
- 1½ teaspoon cinnamon
- 50-75 g raisins
- 100 g chopped nuts
- 4 medium apples, chopped small
- mixing bowls and spoons
- measuring utensils
- 23 x 33 cm cake tin
- paper doily, powdered sugar, sieve
  (optional)

What to do

1 Preheat the oven to 180°C, 350°F, Gas
  Mark 4.

2 Lightly grease the cake tin.

3 Cream the melted butter, syrup or honey
  and vanilla.

4 In another bowl, mix the dry ingredients.

5 Combine the liquid and dry ingredients,
  stirring until blended. Do not over mix; it
  makes the cake dry.

6 Stir in the raisins, nuts and apples.

7 Spread the batter in the cake tin.

8 Bake at 180°C, 350°F, Gas Mark 4 for 45
  minutes or until done.

9 For an extra special occasion, once the
  cake is cool, decorate the top by placing
  a paper doily on top of the cake and
  sifting powdered sugar over the doily.
  Carefully remove the doily, and you
  have a lovely design.

FROM WHEAT TO BREAD

Threshing and winnowing *Age 3+*

Children eat bread everyday, but many have no idea where it comes from. Allowing them to experience the whole "story" of the loaf of bread puts them more closely in touch with nature and gives them a sense of how things are related. The threshing and grinding are activities which can each be done for a series of days. For example, thresh each day for a week, and then grind each day the next week — or even longer! Setting up this activity during free play time allows the children to work while they play.

    NOTE: Do not use treated wheat for any of these activities.

You will need
- wheat on the stalk (available at most garden centres or florists, especially those stocking dried flowers). You can grow it yourself without much difficulty, if you have a sunny garden plot. The stalks of wheat make a lovely autumn display for the season's garden.
- large bowl or basket
- small wooden bowls
- threshing tools — sections of branches about 8 cm and 5 cm in diameter or small round cylindrical wooden blocks
- jar

What to do

1 Show the children how to help you pick the grain heads off the stalks and collect them in a large bowl or basket. Save the wheat straw (stalks) for decorating or add them to the compost heap.

2 Work with two or three children at a time. Put several heads of wheat into a small wooden bowl and give each child a little threshing tool. Show child how to pound the wheat in the bowl with the thresher until all the grains are separated from the stalk and the outer seed covering has come off. The children can winnow the wheat by blowing gently across their bowls to blow the chaff (seed husks) away. The heavier grain should stay in the bottom of the bowl.

3 Pick out the grains and put them in a jar.

4 Continue threshing over a number of days. The children enjoy doing this rhythmic activity again and again. Take turns so that all the children have a turn.

NOTE: An alternative method of threshing wheat that is more like the original way grain was separated from the stalks — using long flails on the threshing floor — is to place the seed heads on a large clean sheet spread on the floor and give four or five children sticks about 60 cm long and 2.5-5 cm in diameter. The children beat the grain rhythmically to separate it from the stalks and to remove its outer covering. Be sure the beating and sticks are carefully controlled. Then another group of children, the "gleaners," pick up the wheat grains before threshing begins again. Now try winnowing the wheat. Gather several hand-fuls of the threshed wheat and place it in a large, flat basket (a large round wooden tray with a 2.5 cm lip also works well) and go outdoors. Toss the wheat a little way up into the air, and the chaff will blow away, leaving you with the heavier grains of wheat. A light breeze makes it work especially well. It's really fun once you get the hang of it, and the children love to watch the chaff fly away.

Grinding flour   *Age 3+*

Now that you have the grist for the mill, you can make flour! Mills are available just for flour, but these are often expensive. A fine alternative is an old-fashioned hand coffee mill. You can also experiment using large smooth stones — one flat and one more rounded. This takes a longer time and produces a coarser flour.

You will need
- a hand coffee mill (see Appendix)
- grains of wheat from the previous activity
- spoon or scoop
- wide-mouthed jar

What to do

1 Put the wheat into the top of the mill with a large spoon or scoop. Hold the mill between your knees to steady it. The children turn the handle to grind the wheat. Usually these mills have a little drawer at the bottom to catch the flour.

2 One child grinds the wheat and pours the ground wheat into a small wide mouth jar. The flour will be a little coarse, but that is fine.

3 The next child fills the mill with the wheat and begins again. Continue until all the wheat is ground, and you have a good supply (a kilo or two) of flour. This activity can continue for several days, or even weeks, during free play time. You can never have too much flour, and the grinder can be positioned significantly in your season's garden.

Baking bread   *Age 3+*

Now, after all the threshing and grinding, you are ready to bake bread. The children can do most of the following, with your help. While the bread bakes, you can tell or read the story of "The Little Red Hen"!

You will need
- 1-2 tablespoons active dry yeast
- 160 ml plus 1 teaspoon honey
- warm water
- 160 ml oil, plus a little extra for greasing the bowl and pan(s)
- 600 g whole wheat flour from the grinding activity, supplemented as needed
- small mixing bowl
- two large bowls
- wooden spoon
- measuring spoons and cups
- wooden board or clean table top
- clean cloth
- two loaf pans or baking trays

What to do

1 In a small bowl, mix the yeast, honey and 125 ml water. Allow this mixture to sit until it gets bubbly — approximately ten minutes.

2 In a large bowl, mix 375 ml warm water, 160 ml oil, 160 ml honey and salt.

3 Pour the yeast mixture into the large bowl and stir in 300 g of whole wheat flour. Mix well, and continue adding more flour until the dough is fairly stiff and not sticky (depending on the humidity, type of flour and so on, you may need to add up to another 300 g of flour).

4 Turn the dough onto a lightly floured board or clean table top and begin to knead, firmly pressing the dough away from you with the heels of your hands, folding it back onto itself and pressing it away from you again. Continue rhythmically kneading the dough until it becomes smooth and elastic. Give the children small balls of dough to knead. Just break off some dough for each child who wants to help, and roll all the pieces back into one big ball when the kneading is finished. They also often like to have a turn kneading the big ball of dough!

5 Place in an oiled bowl, cover with a clean cloth and let rise on a sunny window sill or in another warm place until it doubles in bulk.

6 Punch down (press down two or three times firmly but gently with your fist). Shape into two loaves or 24 rolls (approximately). Cover and let rise once more for about 20-30 minutes.

7 Bake at 180°C, 350°F, Gas Mark 4 for 45-50 minutes for bread or 20 minutes for rolls.

NOTE: You can leave out one rising or both of them (see steps five and six) if you want to eat the bread or rolls for snack the same day. Just ask the children to roll handfuls of dough into balls and place them on an oiled baking tray. Bake them straight away, and you'll have warm, fresh rolls in 20 minutes. Make sure to let them cool a bit before eating. The children love to break the rolls open and watch the steam come out.

PUMPKINS

Carving pumpkins *Age 3+*

Carving pumpkin lanterns is a Hallowe'en tradition. You can also use a turnip but it is much harder to carve. The children can help you to make the lantern a few days before Hallowe'en and you can use it for your celebration centrepiece:

Pumpkin, pumpkin round and fat,
Turn into a lantern just like that!

You will need
- pumpkin
- small, sharp knife
- large spoon
- large bowl
- colander or strainer
- baking tray
- oven
- envelope

What to do

1 Cut a ring around the top of the pumpkin and remove. You may need to cut through strands of pulp to get it off.

2 Show the children how to scoop out the pulp and seeds with a spoon or their hands. Make sure they get the inside of the pumpkin well cleaned. Save the pulp and seeds in a bowl. (NOTE: Always make sure that the children wash their hands thoroughly before handling any food.)

3 Carve a face with two eyes, a nose and a mouth. It's best for young children to have a friendly pumpkin face, so that it is not frightening.

4 Separate the seeds from the pulp. Rinsing the pulp in a colander or wire strainer helps. Place the seeds on the baking tray, keeping a small handful for planting in the garden next spring.

5 Sprinkle some salt on the seeds to be roasted, and bake them in the oven at 180°C, 350°F, Gas Mark 4 for 5-10 minutes or until lightly browned.

6 The seeds you save for planting should be air dried, out of direct sunlight. After a week or so, place them in an envelope, mark with the date and contents and save it in a cool, dry place until spring.

If you would like to have a candle in your pumpkin lantern, use a warming candle or a night light that comes in a little metal cup. They don't tip over easily.

Cooking pumpkins

Age 3+

Now you can turn the pumpkin lantern into cooked pumpkin purée to make a delicious pumpkin pie! Do as much as possible with the children.

You will need
- your lantern and other cleaned pumpkins you want to cook
- sharp knife for the adult
- vegetable peelers
- large pot
- hot plate, stove or electric frying pan
- fork
- food mill
- large bowl

What to do

1 Cut the lantern into large chunks.

2 Ask the children to help you scrape the pumpkin rind off the flesh, using the vegetable peelers.

3 Cut the peeled pumpkin into smaller chunks and place in a pot with about 1 cm of water.

4 Cover and cook over low heat until the pumpkin is soft. Check it by piercing with a fork. Stir occasionally, and add more water if necessary to prevent sticking.

5 Place the food mill over a large bowl, fill with pumpkin and turn the handle to purée the pumpkin.

6 Return the purée to the pot and cook down over a low heat, stirring often. The water should reduce and the purée thicken.

Baking pumpkin pie *Age 3+*

Now you can turn the purée into a pumpkin pie! This is a very, rich pie which makes a very special treat for a harvest celebration.

You will need
- 150 g pumpkin purée
- 125 ml honey
- 2 teaspoons grated orange rind
- $\frac{1}{2}$ teaspoon each of cinnamon and cloves
- $\frac{1}{2}$ teaspoon salt
- $\frac{1}{2}$ teaspoon vanilla
- $\frac{1}{4}$ teaspoon each, nutmeg and ginger
- 2 eggs
- 250 g cream or half milk and half cream
- an unbaked pie shell
- mixing bowl and spoon
- measuring utensils

What to do

1 Prepare an unbaked pie shell with a recipe of your choice, preferably one made with whole wheat flour.

2 Mix the pie ingredients together in a large bowl in the order given.

3 Pour into the pie shell.

4 Bake at 220°C, 425°F, Gas Mark 7 for 45 minutes.

5 The recipe can be doubled to make two pies.

CORN ON THE COB

Removing kernels from the cob *Age 3+*

Corn on the cob can be the source of many harvest activities and a great example of using all the parts of the whole.

You will need
- pieces of corn on the cob (the more the better)
- large wooden bowls or baskets

What to do

1 Take one piece of corn on the cob and remove the husks. Save these in a large basket. They will be used for making dolls in another activity.

2 Hold the fat end of the cob in your hands and begin to push the kernels off with your thumbs. Work over a large wooden bowl or basket that will catch the kernels as they pop off. Continue until the cob is empty.

3 The children love to do this and usually just need you to start it for them by removing a few kernels.

4 Be sure to save all the husks and cobs for other activities.

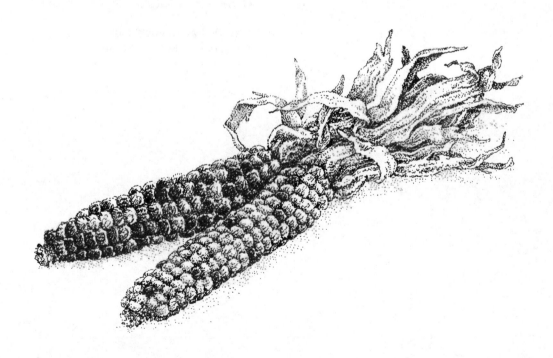

Grinding corn
on the cob   *Age 3+*

Grind the corn with a hand coffee mill, just as you did the wheat flour (see *Grinding flour*, page 49).

You will need
● several cups of kernels of corn on the cob. (If you have soaked the kernels already for the Corn Necklaces, let them dry out for a few days before you try to grind them. If they are too moist, they will gum up the works!)
● hand mill (a coffee grinder works well)
● spoon or scoop
● a jar to store the flour

What to do

1 Put the corn kernels into the top of the mill with a large spoon or scoop. Hold the mill between your knees to steady it. Ask the children to turn the handle to grind the corn. Usually these mills have a little drawer at the bottom to catch the ground corn.

2 Let the children grind the corn and pour the ground corn into a large jar. The flour will be a little coarse, but that is okay.

3 The next child fills the mill with corn and begins again. Continue until you have a good supply of ground corn.

4 Compare the ground corn with ground wheat. It has a different texture, colour and smell.

5 Try grinding the corn with large, smooth stones — one flat, one slightly rounded.

6 When you have a good supply of corn meal, bake some corn muffins.

Baking corn
on the cob   *Age 3+*

Corn bread or corn muffins make a wonderful treat for a harvest celebration, especially when the children have done the grinding and the baking!

You will need
(for twelve muffins)
- 100 g yellow corn meal from the grinding activity, supplemented as needed
- 100 g unbleached white flour
- 1 teaspoon salt
- 3 teaspoons baking powder
- 2 teaspoons sweetener — honey, or syrup
- 250 ml milk
- 1 egg, beaten
- 25 g unsalted butter or margarine, melted, plus extra for greasing the tins
- bun tins or patty tins
- sieve
- mixing bowl and spoon
- measuring utensils

What to do

1 Grease the tins.

2 Sift the dry ingredients into the mixing bowl and then add the sweetener.

3 Add the milk and beaten egg and mix until smooth.

4 Mix in the melted butter.

5 Pour the batter into the tins, almost filling each cup.

6 Bake at 190°C, 375°F, Gas Mark 4 for 12-15 minutes, or until lightly browned.

Making corn husk dolls *Age 4+*

It's good to use up those leftover corn husks by making a doll or doll family (depending on how many husks you have) for the children to play with or to put in your season's garden. The children will enjoy helping you make these.

NOTE: If you would like each child to make a doll, you'll need lots more corn husks, and the children will need help tying the knots.

You will need
- corn husks (saved when you removed the kernels from the cobs)
- pan of warm water
- heavy cotton thread (buttonhole or embroidery thread works well)
- scissors
- stuffing wool or cotton and material scraps for clothes (optional)

What to do

1 Soak the corn husks in warm water for about half an hour.

2 Tie ten husks together tightly at the top.

3 To make the head, tie a neck a short way down from the top. You can stuff a little wool or cotton in here if you like.

4 Separate three husks on both sides, and tie them halfway down for the arms. Trim away the excess.

5 To make the body, tie the remaining husks just above half way down.

6 Make legs by tying five husks on each side, a bit up from the ends. Trim the ends.

7 Add clothing — scarves, hats, shawls, skirts, jackets, and so on.

Stringing corn necklaces   *Age 4 +*

These necklaces are easy to make and fun for children to have as autumn jewellery.

You will need
- corn on the cob
- large bowl
- water
- long strands of heavy cotton thread (buttonhole or embroidery thread)
- heavy sewing needles
- sellotape and pen

What to do

1 Soak a large quantity of the corn kernels in a bowl of water overnight. It's fun for the children to help you set this up the day before you plan to string the necklaces. If you plan to grind the corn (see *Grinding corn on the cob,* page 54), save several cups of kernels for that — they will grind more easily if they haven't been soaked first.

2 In the morning, pour off the water and bring the bowl of corn to the work table. The children love to dip their hands in and "finger" the damp corn that has softened and swelled a bit overnight.

3 Give each child a needle double threaded with 60 cm of thread. Tie a knot about 5 cm from the end. Using doubled thread will keep the needles from coming unthreaded.

4 The children choose the kernels they want, push the needle through the centre of each kernel (be careful for little fingers here) and slide the kernel down to the knot. It's helpful to start with the kernel resting on the table.

5 The children thread as many (or as few) kernels as they want, again leaving about 5 cm of string at the other end. To continue this activity over a few days, just mark each string with the child's name and keep the unused corn kernels moist by covering them with a damp towel and refrigerating them so they don't get mouldy.

6 When the necklaces are finished, centre the corn kernels if they don't have a full string and tie the open ends together in a bow around the children's necks.

7 Some of the corn may begin to sprout — a perfect opportunity to grow some corn plants indoors to be transplanted to your garden in the spring. Then harvest your own corn on the cob next autumn.

Grating corn cobs

Age 3+

This is a very simple activity which the children enjoy doing, and which often occupies them during free play. The rhythmic grating is fun and can absorb the children for long periods of time.

You will need
- corn on the cob
- bowls

What to do

1 Set up this activity in the play area.

2 Show the children how when two cobs are "grated" together — that is, one is rubbed against the other — a fine, flaky powder is produced to save in bowls for "cooking."

NOTE: The children will probably find lots of other uses for the corn cobs, and they will become a regular part of play.

2 Winter

The season's garden in winter

For more detailed information on setting up a season's garden, see page 23.

Winter colours: soft greens and blues, browns, white.

Special objects: attractive rocks and stones: crystals; branches of evergreens, placed in a vase of water as you would flowers; a white candle, even if you can't light it; star-shaped seed pods; tiny brass stars or stars cut from gold paper.

Wreath: Remove the autumn decorations from your wreath. Gather evergreen branches and transform the wreath one day, with the children's help, by binding the evergreens over the straw base. Use dark coloured cord or heavy string to hold the evergreens in place. Using a pretty ribbon to hang the wreath also makes it more festive. Be sure to "water" the wreath daily with a plant mister to keep it from getting too dry.

Plantings: Carefully gather moss from an outdoor area (a damp area like a river bed or the ground near the north side of trees) and transplant it in your dish garden (a large clay plant saucer). You don't have to fill the garden, even a small mossy area is nice. Mist it occasionally. Tuck in little stones and pieces of bark or tiny pine-cones.

Special Activity: Force narcissus bulbs, available at garden or hardware shops. Just two or three of these lovely blooms will perfume your whole room. They are easy to grow in a small dish of pebbles. Nestle the bottoms of the bulbs in the pebbles. Pour in enough water so that the bottoms of the bulbs are always wet, and replenish the water as necessary. I used a dish of bulbs on the meal table — a lively centrepiece. Start the bulbs about two to three weeks before you would like them to bloom.

"Real toys"

Opportunities for playing outside during winter are limited by the weather, but we can still bring the natural world into homes and classrooms in the form of "real toys" from nature.

Pre-school-aged children are blessed with very active imaginations. For them, play is work, and through creative play, they learn about the world and how to live in the world. We can support this process of exploring and growing by providing children with toys and materials that can grow with them. Nature provides us with many of these materials — free for the collecting. Ideas for providing "real toys" are given in the Introduction on page 18.

NOTE: Be sure that when you gather things from nature, such as this moss, that you take only a little from any one area, so as not to deplete the "stock" in that area. Also, remove it carefully and refill or tamp down the area so that you don't leave scars. Your own attitude of care and reverence towards the natural world will mean a lot to children, and they will imitate it.

ACTIVITIES AND CRAFTS

Caring for the birds and squirrels   *Age 3+*

Caring for the birds (and other wild creatures) is a way of bringing nature very close to your home or classroom — especially in more urban areas. The regular responsibility of caring for and feeding the birds each day is very rewarding for the children and develops good habits.

You will need
- bird seed (often available in bulk from hardware shops and garden centres
- bird feeders (this can range from something you make or buy to a flat tree stump or window sill)
- bird bath — a large shallow pan, dish or large plant saucer works as well as the standard bird bath. It is better to place it down on the ground or on a low stump than to have it up on a pedestal. This makes it more accessible to the children for filling and cleaning.
- nuts in shells
- corn on the cob (for the squirrels to eat, but they may also enjoy your bird seed)
- large, thick nails
- small brush
- large fruit juice container or plastic jug and string (optional)

What to do

1 Find a place within view of your windows to set up the feeding station. It may be a window sill if you're not on the ground floor. In this case, a bird feeder that attaches to the window with suction cups may be best. Or you can attach a small board to the window sill.

2 Birds like a protected area, so place a bush or tree (container plantings will work) in the feeding area outside your windows.

3 Hang the feeder there or place the seed on the ground or on a tree stump. Place the nuts for the squirrels on the ground or on a low stump or flat rock nearby. If you are feeding the squirrels corn on the cob, drive a large, thick nail into the stump and press the flat end of the corn cob down onto the nail head to hold it upright. The squirrels will also appreciate left over apple cores and carrot tops, and they'll love your roasted pumpkin seeds. Place the water dish or bird bath nearby. Just strive to make it a pleasant place for the birds and the squirrels to be. Add plants, rocks and so on, to make the setting more natural.

4 Each morning one of the children can help you fill the feeder(s) with seed, put out some nuts and corn and replenish the water supply. Free play time is a good time to do this, and the children love to help. The bird bath should be emptied, scrubbed with a small brush (no soap) and rinsed once a week. This is another favourite job and a chance for some water play.

5 If the birds and the squirrels don't come straight away, keep putting out the food and be patient. They will find it soon. (NOTE: One way to attract birds is with the sound of water. Punch a small hole in a large fruit juice container or a plastic jug, fill it with water and hang it above the bird bath so that the water will drip into it.)

6 Birds and squirrels are often the wildest creatures that children get to see other than the animals in the zoo. Caring for them regularly is a simple way of helping the children feel a connection to nature and a responsibility for its well-being, particularly in the winter months when the animals have a harder time finding their own food. If you live in an area where it gets cold, just wait for that first "real" winter day when there is ice in the bird bath!

Pine-cone bird feeders *Age 3+*

These are easy to make and the birds love them!

You will need
- pine-cones (long ones work best, but any kind will do)
- peanut butter (the cheapest sugarless kind you can find — some natural food shops buy it in bulk, so you can buy as much or as little as you want. You will probably be able to make approximately twelve pine-cone bird feeders per half-kilo of peanut butter.)
- bird seed (the least expensive kind you can find)
- a baking sheet or large plate to hold the seed
- heavy string, twine or yarn
- ice lolly or craft sticks or tongue depressors
- grease-proof paper

What to do

1 Apply the peanut butter to the pine-cone with the craft sticks, pressing it into all the nooks and crannies. Expect that fingers will be licked and some peanut butter will be eaten. Just remind the children that this snack is really for the birds!

2 Roll the peanut butter covered pine-cone into a pan of bird seed. The bird seed will stick to the peanut butter. Gently shake off the excess.

3 Tie the string or yarn tightly around the base or top of the pine-cone.

4 If you are doing this at school the children could make two pine-cone bird feeders — one for school and one for home. Then you will have a supply to use at school and the children will be able to see how they work to attract the birds. The children will take them home enthusiastically!

5 It's better to wrap them in grease-proof paper as this is a lot less sticky than cling-film (besides being less burden on the environment).

Star windows   *Age 3+*

These little windows of coloured light, made from tissue-paper transparencies, are a special addition to a window near your season's garden. They also create a seasonal mood, depending on the colours and forms you choose. To the children, they are magical when placed on the window so that the sunlight shines through.

You will need
- sugar paper or card — deep red and blue
- coloured tissue-paper — golds, yellows and white (see Appendix)
- scissors
- basket or tray
- white glue, small saucers and cotton swabs or glue sticks

What to do

1 Cut the sugar paper or card into frames in the shape of your choice. A plain rectangle with rounded edges to soften the shape is fine; a star would be extra special, but will take longer to do. The total size is up to you, but make it no smaller than 15 cm long and 10 cm wide. The frame edge itself should be approximately 2-2.5 cm thick. (NOTE: You can also cut the frame on a fold. This will give you a hinged frame. Glue the white tissue to the inside top and show the children glue on their stars. Then glue the sides of the frame together and you have a very nicely finished star window.)

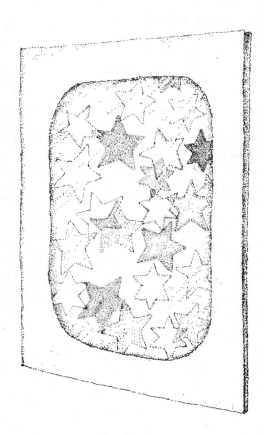

2 Run a bead of glue all around the back of the frame near the outer edge and press a large piece of white tissue-paper over it. Trim the tissue-paper.

3 Cut the yellow and gold tissue-paper into star shapes, in varying sizes if you like. By folding the tissue accordion style, you can cut many stars at the same time. Place the stars in a basket or on a tray.

4 Write the children's names on the back of the frame (the side with the tissue-paper glued on). This is the side on which they work.

5 Give each child a glue stick or ask them to share a small dish or saucer of glue (just put a little on the dish). They could use a cotton swab to apply the glue, but use these sparingly as they cannot be re-used.

6 Using a *tiny* drop of glue for each star, the children cover the white tissue with stars. Encourage them to fill the surface, although younger ones may just place a few stars on the tissue-paper. It is fine to overlap the stars, as this creates interesting shapes and beautiful and surprising new colours.

7 When they have finished, add an extra covering of white tissue as you did in step two. This isn't necessary, but provides a nice protective backing and gives the transparency a more finished look.

8 Let the children hold them up to the light. They are always captivated by the results.

9 Cover your home or classroom windows with star windows.

NOTE: This technique for making tissue-paper transparencies is endlessly variable. The frames can be cut into any shape, from apples or pumpkins (autumn) to eggs (spring). Just choose the tissue-paper in seasonal colours and cut the sugar paper or card into appropriate shapes. Generally, white tissue-paper is used for backing in all cases.

Snow scenes   *Age 3+*

Here's a chance to play with "snow" indoors without a mess, and to create something lasting and beautiful.

You will need
- pieces of fairly sturdy, smooth cardboard cut into rounded, irregularly shaped pieces, approximately 10 x 6 cm (one piece per child)
- pen
- fine grain pure soap powder
- mixing bowl
- rotary egg beater (hand-operated type)
- spoon
- natural objects — small stones or crystals, bits of bark or tiny sticks, tiny winter leaves, acorns or acorn caps, holly berries or cranberries, tiny bits of evergreen, and so on. Sort these into bowls or baskets.
- beeswax (optional)

What to do

1 Place about 250 g of soap powder in the mixing bowl and add about 180 ml water. Beat until the mixture holds stiff peaks; do not over beat. It should be the consistency of whipped cream. This amount should make enough "snow" for ten to twelve pieces of cardboard, depending on size. Let the children help with the measuring, pouring and beating.

2 Write each child's name on the underside of his or her cardboard, and let the children choose a few objects with which to create their snow scenes. Mound one to two heaping tablespoonfuls of "snow" onto the cardboard base and spread it out a bit.

3 Press the sticks, stones and so on, gently down into the snow, one at a time. Guide the children a bit so that they are creating a woodland scene and not just a jumble. For example, a stick becomes a log onto which a little red beeswax bird could perch. Then a bit of evergreen, a stone and a pine-cone or acorn can be grouped around it. The idea is not to see how many things can fit on the cardboard, but to choose a few objects and place them carefully.

4 Let the snow scenes sit undisturbed for one hour. If you have whipped in too much air, they may need to dry overnight (they will have the consistency of marshmallows).

5 Cut a larger piece of cardboard and make a children's scene to place in your season's garden. A small mirror placed down in the snow becomes an icy pond, a larger mound of snow a hill for sledging. Create skaters, children sledging, snowball throwers and snowmen with coloured beeswax. You might even fashion one from the snow. The older children could work on this for days.

NOTE: For information on moulding and shaping beeswax, see the instructions in *Beeswax modelling,* page 86.

Nutmeg grating   *Age 3+*

Children love to grate things. Start with whole nutmeg which will make the room smell like a wonderful spice shop. They will then want to try to grate other things, so let them. Save avocado stones for them to use, and corn cobs work well too. The spice gratings can be saved for baking or potpourri. The corn cob and avocado gratings are great for "cooking" and eventually end up in the compost.

You will need
- nutmeg graters (they are inexpensive and are available from kitchen and hardware shops)
- grating materials (whole nutmeg, corn cobs, avocado stones and whatever else you or the children imagine trying)
- bowls
- covered containers

What to do

1 Place the grating materials and little graters in the kitchen along with bowls to grate into.

2 You may not even need to show the children what to do — just stand back and watch.

3 Put out covered containers to save the gratings from day to day. If you are doing this at school, you may want to let the children take some home; they will probably want to. The children in my class liked to wrap little packages of grated nutmeg in paper towels. It was like gold dust to them.

Finger knitting   *Age 4+*

This might more appropriately be called finger crochet as the result is a lovely woollen chain that can be made into many things or used as is. Working with warm woollen yarn is a nice wintertime activity, and finger knitting is a pleasant way to pass time indoors. The rhythmic pulling of the yarn can be quite calming.

You will need
- bulky wool — ask at your local wool shop for 100% wool, bulky weight yarn. Try to get real wool rather than acrylic, as the wool comes from nature instead of a laboratory and has a much nicer, warmer feel. It's also more pleasant to work with. The younger the children, the thicker the wool should be. You could also use cotton yarn, but it tends not to slide so easily (see Appendix).
- a basket or cloth sack for each child's work

What to do

1 Cut long lengths of wool (four to five arm lengths), and show the children how to roll them into balls. Give each child a small handwork basket or cloth sack marked with his or her name in which the projects "in process" can be kept. This keeps the materials organized and lets the children work on the projects for days at a time.

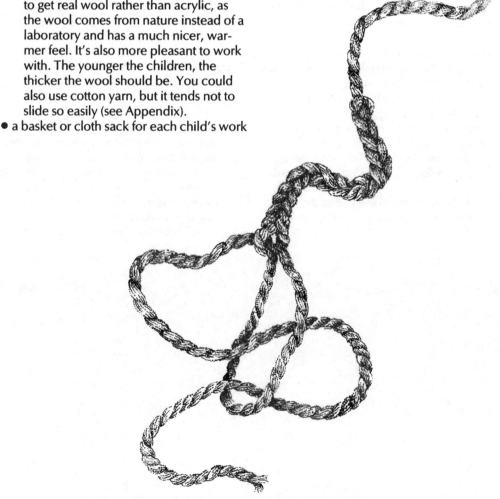

2 Start the finger knitting by making a slip knot. Lay one end of the wool across your open palm and hold the end down with your thumb. Wrap the wool once around your fingers and cross over the first piece. Hold it down again with your thumb. Now you have a loop around your fingers. Bring the long side of the wool back through this loop to make a second loop, and while still holding the short end of the wool, pull the second loop up. This will tighten the first loop. If the second loop gets too long and unwieldy, just pull on the long side of the loop to make the loop smaller.

3 Continue finger knitting by reaching down through the loop to pull the wool strand up through the loop. Always hold the finger-knitted strand firmly and near the open loop. Sometimes it helps to have a little verse to help the children remember what to do. Here's a suggestion:
   Reach into the lake, (The open loop)
   Catch a fish to bake. (Pull up the wool)

4 When you get close to the end of the wool, pull the end up through the loop to knot it off.

5 If you have a particular finished length in mind, start finger knitting with approximately four to five times that length.

6 The resulting knit "ropes" can be used for free play in many different ways. We kept a basket full of them on our shelf, and they were used for horse reins (place the centre of the rope at the back of the neck, bring the two ends to the front, cross the ends and bring them under the armpits to the back); hoses for fire fighters; ties for cloth capes and other clothing; for "wrapping" presents; for building houses, making gates, and so on. They are very useful.

7 You can also use the finger knitting to make more conventional items. They make perfect mitten strings. Stitch one end to each one of a pair of mittens or gloves. Run the string through the child's coat sleeves — no more lost mittens! A very attractive rug can be made by coiling the finger knitting and stitching it together to make a round braided-type rug. If you have a playhouse or doll's house you could put one there or you could be very ambitious and make one for your story corner!

Sewing dwarves   *Age 3+*

Sewing is a wonderful wintertime activity and is suited to a variety of ages. The younger children may sew a stitch or two and go off to something else. The older ones may want to stitch lots of dwarves. Perhaps they would like to make seven in different rainbow colours and a Snow White to go with them. Sewing is a wonderful quietening activity and can be helpful for children who are at a loose end or in need of calming down. Just bring them to the sewing table, sit them down and get them started.

You will need
- felt with a high wool content — it is much softer than the acrylic kind which is often thin and feels quite stiff. Get a variety of colours: red, yellow, green, blue, violet, and so on (see Appendix).
- large eye needles
- thread
- scissors
- pins
- wool or cotton batting for stuffing (see Appendix)
- baskets or bags

What to do

1 Place the dwarf pattern on a piece of folded felt and cut. You can make the pattern larger or smaller to create dwarves of different sizes. The older children can cut their own by pinning the pattern to a small square of felt.

2 Thread the needles with doubled thread, about 30 cm long (that would be 60 cm to start with), and tie a knot at the end of the thread. This will keep the thread on the needles, and prevent you from having to keep rethreading needles.

3 Using an over-stitch (over the top edge of the material), sew from the top of the pointy hat down to the rounded face opening, knot and cut the thread.

4 Re-knot the thread, and sew the body of the dwarf.

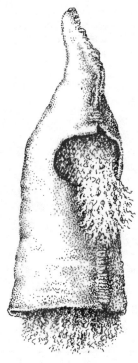

5 Stuff generously with stuffing wool or cotton so the dwarf feels firm. You can pull down a bit of wool from the bottom of the "face" to make a beard.

6 Don't expect the younger ones to do a perfect job. They will eventually improve their sewing skills by imitating you and the older children. Let them do what they are able to do, and help them if they need help. You can help to undo any drastic mistakes.

7 The older children may want to make more than one dwarf. Keep the dwarves in the children's handwork baskets or bags, and the children can work on them for several days or weeks. This project could last throughout the winter.

Tissue-paper dolls

Age 4+

The children can complete their set of dwarves with a tissue-paper doll — Snow White, perhaps. This method of making the dolls can be modified for many different occasions by using different colours. The children may want to make several.

You will need
- tissue-paper (white or different colours)
- wool or cotton stuffing
- string or strong thread

What to do

1 Cut tissue-paper into two rectangles — one 10 x 20 cm, and the other 7.5 x 15 cm. Use one colour for both pieces or vary the colours.

2 Show the children how to form a bit of stuffing wool into a small tight ball about 2 cm in diameter. This will be for the head.

3 Place the ball just about half way down the larger tissue-paper rectangle and fold the tissue over it, gathering it where the neck should be.

4 Place the smaller tissue-paper rectangle over the top of the head side to side and also gather this tissue-paper around the neck, leaving the front open — this will be the face.

5 Help the children tie the thread (use it doubled if it's not strong) around the neck, knotting at the back of the head.

6 Twist the two sides of the smaller rectangle into arms and hands. The back will look like a small cape.

7 Fluff out the skirt so the figure will stand.

NOTE: You may add a bit of coloured fleece for hair before putting on the smaller rectangle, and you can put just a drop of glue on the places where the skirt comes together at each side to keep these from separating.

Wool dolls　　*Age 4+*

These little dolls are very easy to make. The children will just need your help with tying knots.

You will need
- firm cardboard (corrugated works best) cut into 8 x 12 cm pieces
- medium weight wool in assorted colours (thinner wool also works, but thick wool is too bulky for this craft project)
- scissors
- fabric scraps, safety pins (optional)

What to do

1 Measure out approximately four arm lengths (about 3.5 metres) of yarn and show the children how to roll it into a little ball. You will need one for each doll.

2 Give each child a piece of cardboard and a little ball of wool. Show them how to wrap all the wool around the cardboard. Wind the wool around the long way for a bigger doll (almost 12 cm tall) or around the width for a smaller doll.

3 Slide a short piece of wool under the wrappings to gather them, and tie them tightly together.

4 Now slide the wrapped wool off the cardboard. The tie will hold it together.

5 Take a small piece of wool and tie the bundle tightly where the neck should be. This creates the head.

6 Separate about a quarter of the strands of wool to the left and a quarter to the right to form the arms (just do it by sight, it needn't be exact). Tie each of these smaller bundles where the wrist should be and trim away the excess. Don't make the arms too long.

7 Tie around the body bundle at the place where the waist should be. If you want to make a doll with a skirt, you can stop here. If you want to make a figure wearing trousers, separate the body bundle into two bunches, tying each off at the ankle. Trim the ends.

8 Let the children help as much as possible with the knot tying. They can also help with the trimming.

9 Older children may wish to add clothes: scarves, shawls, belts... This is a great way to use up fabric scraps.

10 The 8 cm and 12 cm dolls make attractive additions to a toy collection and are useful when the children are building farms, villages and so on, to "people" their scenes. They may want to make several dolls. They are so simple that they leave lots of room for the imagination.

11 The smaller dolls also make sweet gifts as decorative brooches. Just add a safety pin to the back, and you can pin them on hats, coats, and so on.

GIFT MAKING

Wooden candleholders *Age 3+*

These are really quite simple to make once you've gathered the materials. They are very beautiful and very practical, too. If you have made your own candles (see *Candle dipping,* page 87, and *Rolling candles,* page 89), put them in the holders, wrap them in a big sheet of tissue-paper — a lovely and useful gift!

You will need
- slices of small logs or branches — one per child — approximately 8-10 cm in diameter and with a 2 cm hole drilled in the centre of each slice. (Perhaps you can get a carpenter or local woodworking shop to do the cutting and hole drilling for you.)
- marker
- white or yellow glue (yellow carpenter's glue works very well)
- an assortment of small things from nature: tiny pine-cones (spruce), acorns or acorn caps, tiny shells, small seed pods, nuts (especially hazelnuts) and cranberries (these provide a beautiful splash of colour). Use anything that's not too large.
- bird seed and spoon (optional)

What to do

1 Write each child's name on the underside of the candleholder.

2 Spread the glue, fairly thickly, all over the top of the candleholder, taking care not to get it in the hole that will hold the candle. The glue will dry clear.

3 The children choose natural objects and place them all over the top of the candleholders, pressing them down into the glue. Encourage the children to cover the top. If you want, you can sprinkle a spoonful of bird seed all over the top of the candleholder when the children have finished to fill in any spaces or holes.

4 Place the candleholder somewhere out of the way to dry.

5 If you are making candles — either dipping, rolling or decorating — wait until those are done and then each one can be placed in its own holder.

Herbal sachets *Age 3+*

These sachets are easy to make and are
useful, beautiful gifts. Don't be too concerned about the quality of the sewing — it's
thought and effort that count here. These can
also be a nice Valentine's Day gift by cutting
red felt into heart shapes.

You will need
- paper (for the pattern)
- felt (with a high wool content) in assorted
  colours (see Appendix)
- scissors
- pins
- sewing thread in matching or contrasting
  colours
- large eye needles
- sachet mix or potpourri — available in
  many places. Try to choose a pleasant
  smelling one that is not too overpower-
  ing. You can also make your own by
  choosing interesting looking and smelling herbs. I like to combine lavender,
  dried rose buds and star anise (a spice)

all of which are interesting, beautiful to
look at and smell good! These are also
easier to handle as they are (except for
the lavender) larger and less flaky. Try
herb and spice shops or gift shops. To
stretch the sachet materials, mix them
with wool or cotton batting.

What to do

1 For each child cut out two hearts, or
  whatever other shapes you want to use,
  for each sachet. Cutting the shape on a
  fold will insure that the shape will be
  symmetrical. Older children can help cut
  by pinning the folded pattern to a folded
  piece of felt. The illustration shows the
  actual size.

2 Pin the two (front and back) pieces together
  with a straight pin. Double thread a
  needle and tie a knot in the thread ends.

3 Start the sewing by bringing the needle through the fabric from the inside so that the knot will not show. Show the children how to sew around the edge using any kind of stitch. I found that a simple over-stitch which goes through the fabric and then over the top is easiest for the children to do. Its greatest problems are stitches too far apart or, too tight which makes a crinkle at the edge of the fabric (this requires mending only in extreme circumstances). Help the children to keep the stitches fairly small and close together so the sachet mix won't leak out. This is another reason for using a sachet mix with large chunks of things rather than a really flaky or powdery mix.

4 Ask the children to stop sewing when there is about 2.5-3 cm left to sew, so that they can stuff their sachet.

5 Stuff with the sachet mix (and wool if you are using it), and let the children finish their sewing. You can also stitch a piece of thin ribbon to the top (or let the children finger knit a cord) to make the sachet into a necklace.

6 When they reach the end (where they began sewing), knot off the thread and check to see that there are no gaping holes around the edges that need repair.

7 The children can wrap the finished sachets in coloured tissue-paper and present them as Valentine's Day gifts.

Pompon balls   *Age 3+*

Fun and easy to make, and fun to play with. The addition of a tiny brass bell or jingle bell makes them extra special gifts. This is another project that the children can work on over a period of days.

You will need
- wool — bulky weight (thick) is best for 10 cm balls. If you use medium weight wool, the wrapping takes longer.
- basket
- cardboard
- large scissors
- wool needle
- medium to large size jingle bells or little brass bells
- heavy thread (buttonhole or embroidery)

What to do

1 Prepare the wool by cutting it into arm length strands. Keep these in a basket.

2 Cut two ring doughnut-shaped forms from the cardboard for each pompon. You can share the forms, letting one child use them after another has finished. Cut a slit in each form. This will allow you to slide the pompon off when you are done, so the form can be re-used.

3 Give the children a set (two) of cardboard forms and an arm's length of wool. Use a variety of colours to suit your situation. Seasonal colours are lovely for gifts. You can make them just one colour, or let the children choose completely and have confetti-coloured "pot luck" pompons!

4 Show the children how to wrap their wool around the form going through the centre hole and around the "doughnut" part of the form. Show them how to wrap the first strand by holding it in place. When they've finished wrapping the strand of wool, they should tuck the end under the wrapped ones to keep it from unravelling.

5 Continue wrapping the strands of wool until the centre hole of the doughnut is completely filled up. It will be hard to push the wool through at the end. Tuck the last end under the other strands.

6 Using a large sharp pair of scissors, cut around the outside edge of the pompons, keeping one blade between the two cardboard forms.

7 Using heavy thread or doubled wool, tie the pompon tightly through the middle of the two pieces of cardboard.

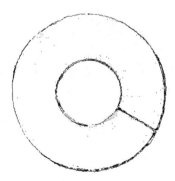

8 Slide the wool off the form through the slits.

9 Fluff up and trim the pompon. Save the trimmings for use as stuffing.

10 To add a bell, thread a wool needle with doubled wool, run it through the bell's loop and then run the needle back through its own wool to anchor the bell to the wool. Then thread the needle up through the centre of the pompon. Pull snugly, so the bell nestles in, cut the thread and knot it so that it forms a large loop. These can be used to decorate the Christmas tree. Or if they are hung on a door knocker or doorknob at holiday time, they can cheerfully announce the arrival of guests.

Pomanders   *Age 3+*

These clove-studded fruits make useful gifts and are fun to make. They are natural air fresheners and can be hung in a cupboard where they will delicately scent the air for up to a year.

This project can be varied according to the age of the children. Five year olds should be able to make them by themselves. Three year olds may need the holes punched for them. Perhaps, rather than each child making their own, younger children can help with a shared pomander to hang in the bathroom or in a sunny window.

You will need
- oranges, lemons or apples
- pins or small nails
- whole cloves
- spice mixture (ground cinnamon, allspice, cardamon, cloves — mix your own combination)
- wool or ribbon for hanging

What to do

1 If necessary, use the nail or pin to puncture holes in the skin of the fruit about 5 mm apart.

2 Press the whole cloves into the holes, working to cover the entire skin of the fruit. Make sure you leave room (a narrow gap between the cloves will be fine) for the wool or ribbon. This is a stage which can be done over several days.

3 When the entire fruit is studded with cloves, roll the fruit in the spice mixture.

4 Twist two pieces of wool or ribbon together at the middle and place the pomander over the twist. Take the four ends, tie them together in a firm knot, and then make a pretty bow.

Pine-cone fire lighters   *Age 3+*

These are simple and easy to make. They make wonderful gifts for anyone with a wood-burning stove or open fireplace, and they really work!

You will need
- pine-cones (any kind will do, although the longer, thinner ones work best)
- wool, ribbon or heavy thread
- wax (beeswax scraps or used candle ends are fine but you can use the less expensive paraffin wax, or a mixture of both)
- grease-proof paper

What to do

1 Read the procedure for dipping candles, as this works much the same way (see *Candle dipping,* page 87).

2 Melt the wax as for dipping candles.

3 Tie a string or piece of wool or ribbon around the bottom of each pine-cone. Make a loop about 10 cm long at the end of the pine-cone.

4 Holding the end of the string, dip the pine-cone slowly into the melted wax. Then hold it above the can for a few seconds until it stops dripping. Repeat two more times. Then lay it on a piece of grease-proof paper to harden.

5 Tie the string into a bow at the top, or tie three or four pine-cones into a bundle. Keep them until the gift giving time approaches. You can wrap them in tissue-paper if you like.

INSTRUCTIONS FOR USE: Place the fire lighters in the fireplace and light them with kindling to start a fire.

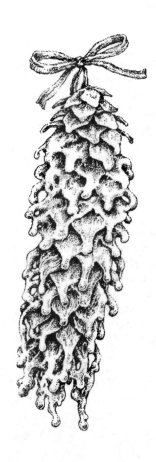

Stained glass triptych *Age 4+*

This is an extra special version of the *Star windows* (see page 64) and uses the same techniques. These triptychs make wonderful holiday gifts.

You will need

- coloured sugar paper or watercolour paper, card stock or posterboard for the frames
- scissors
- tissue-paper (white and coloured)
- white glue or glue sticks
- pen

What to do

1 Make the frames by cutting the three-sided form (see illustration) from paper or posterboard. The approximate measurement for the centre section is 15 cm high and 13 cm wide. The side measurements are 10 cm high and 8 cm wide. This will just fit across a 21 x 30 cm (A4) sheet of paper.

2 Cut out a "window" from the centre section leaving a 2 cm frame. You can also cut windows in the side frames.

3 Glue a piece of white tissue-paper over the back of the window opening(s).

4 Give the children their frames and, working on the back side, have them *tear* small pieces, approximately the size of a 10p piece, of coloured tissue-paper and glue them to the white window. Encourage them to fill the entire surface. They may overlap pieces as this creates new forms and colours. The tearing creates soft edges rather than hard lines and gives a very attractive effect. Just take care that the pieces are not too large, and that they use small amounts of glue. You can control the colours offered to suit a particular theme or to insure a pleasant mix.

5 When they have filled the window with colour, write their name on the back, fold back the two side supports and stand the triptych on the window sill so they can see the sunlight shine through. These are very attractive when used carefully with a warming candle or night light (the kind that comes in its own little glass holder) behind the centre window. The children are captivated by the beautiful coloured light.

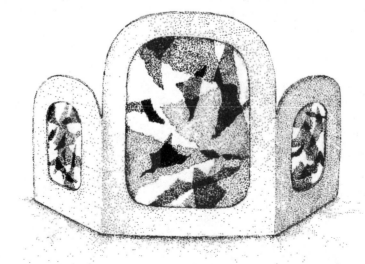

Folded paper boxes   *Age 5+*

These can be made in any size depending on how big a piece of paper you begin with. They are very handy for little gifts and treasures, and a set of three that nest one inside the other is lots of fun to open.

You will need
- heavy weight paper (watercolour paper works best. Sugar paper will also work, but the box just won't be as sturdy.)
- scissors
- glue or tape
- crayons or watercolour paints and brushes (optional)

What to do

1 If the paper is white, you may want to let the children colour or paint it first. Watercolour painted boxes can be quite beautiful.

2 Take the paper and fold one corner up along the opposite edge. Trim away any excess. This gives you a perfect square to start. Now fold the other bottom corner up to the opposite corner. These two folds intersect at the centre of the square. Establishing this centre point is important for the other folds.

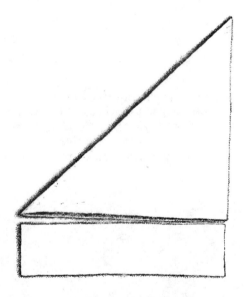

3 One at a time, place the tip of each corner of the square at the centre point and make a crease. This gives you folds which look like a large square composed of four smaller squares in the centre of your paper.

4 Again, using the tip of each corner, fold over to the opposite edge of the large square. Now almost the entire paper is made up of square folds.

5 Fold the tip of each corner just to the first folded line near it. This gives you a little triangular tip at each corner.

6 Find the central square. It will be composed of four smaller squares. This is the bottom of your box. Cut along the folded lines of two of the opposite sides toward the centre, just to the edge of this centre square.

7 Starting at the tips you did not cut, fold two opposite sides over and in until you reach the bottom centre of the square. Leave these folded sides standing to make two sides of the box. Then fold the wing-like edges of the sides around so that they overlap and make the other two sides.

8 Now finish the box. Fold the remaining two tips in, bringing them up and over the sides and pressing the tip down along the bottom inside of the box. You can put a drop of glue or a small loop of tape under each of these tips to hold them in place. A box!

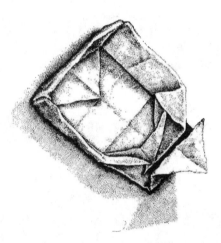

NOTE: Make sure to crease all your folds well — the box will be better for it. The children can help with the original decorating, but the folding needs to be pretty precise. To see the final box emerge is a wonder for them!

BEESWAX

Beeswax modelling *Age 3+*

Beeswax is just what it says it is — a truly natural modelling material. Talk to the children about the work of the bees who make it in their busy colonies.

Beeswax is perfect for young children as it warms in the hands and becomes more pliable as you use it. It's not cold to the touch and doesn't dry out like clay. It comes in colours, smells delightful and is very economical because it can be re-used over and over and a little bit goes a long way. It comes in small slabs and is available through mail order, although you could ask your local toy or art shop to order it.

You will need
- modelling beeswax, cut into small pieces about 2.5 cm square (see Appendix)
- a small cake tin or baking tray
- a basket or plastic bag

What to do

1 If it is very cold weather, you may want to warm the beeswax gently by putting the little pieces in a small cake tin or baking tray and sitting them near a heat source.

2 Give each child one small piece to start. Suggest that they put it in their "little ovens" (their closed hands) to warm and soften it.

3 Begin to manipulate the beeswax with your fingers, kneading, pulling, pushing and rubbing it. Stretch it out so thin that you can see the light shine through.

4 At first it's good to just get to know the material, not making anything in particular. Just play with it. You may want to do just this much several times.

5 Make various objects by warming the beeswax, working it to make it flexible and then shaping it into various forms, from birds to baskets to people. You might set up a little scene — some pine-cones on a green cloth, a few rocks — and tell a story about the birds who live in this "forest." While you're telling — and after — the children can be making the birds, or whatever, to place in the forest. Send each bird home with its maker, or re-soften the wax and form it into little beeswax patties to be used another time. Store in a basket or plastic bag.

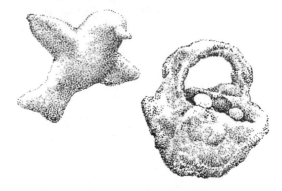

NOTE: You may also want to control the colour selection at first, using only one colour at a time, as this reduces colour competition among the children and keeps the individual pieces a pure colour. Older children may ask to use different colours to make hair, clothes, tree trunks, flowers, animals, and so on. Younger ones should do quite well with one colour at a time.

Candle dipping   *Age 4+*

Pure beeswax makes the most beautiful candles. It is very fragrant and nice to work with, but may be expensive.

This activity gives the children a chance to see a candle take shape, which is very magical to them. The candles also make wonderful gifts alone or in a candleholder (see *Wooden candleholders,* page 75).

This activity may seem complicated, but once you do it and see that it isn't so hard and is so much fun, you'll want to repeat it every year.

You will need

- candle wicking — available at craft shops. Don't be tempted to use string; it's worth getting the real thing if you want the candles to burn well. The candles will probably end up being about 2.5 cm in diameter, so get the right size wicking (see Appendix.)
- masking tape and pen
- pure beeswax (you can mix it with less expensive paraffin wax if need be)
- towel, rubber or wooden mallet, and screwdriver
- two tall narrow round containers (perhaps fruit juice tins) cleaned and with tops removed
- a large pot (you'll need a pot big enough to hold the two containers in a water bath)
- hot plate or stove
- newspaper
- potholders
- grease-proof paper

What to do

1 Cut the wicking into pieces about 25-30 cm long.

2 Using a tab of masking tape, mark each wick at one end with the name of a child. This will prevent confusion after the candles are dipped.

3 The beeswax usually comes in large, thick chunks and needs to be broken into smaller pieces to fit in the cans for melting. I put the beeswax on a towel on the floor, and use a mallet (or block of wood) and screwdriver to break it up by gently driving the tip of the screwdriver through the piece near the edge. The children love to help with the hammering and gathering of the pieces, so if you have the time, do this with the children on the day before you want to dip candles. Tell the children that the fragrant wax is a gift from the bees!

4 About an hour or so before you want to make the candles, begin to melt the wax. Fill the containers half to three-quarters full with beeswax chips and pieces and place the containers in the pot almost filled with water. Experiment with the amount of water to put in the pot, as you don't want the containers to float and tip over. Usually you can get the water deep enough to come about halfway up the sides of the container. The higher the water, the faster the wax will melt, but again, you don't want the containers to tip over. A small deep pot works better than a wide shallow one. (NOTE: Take care to make this area off limits to the children and have an adult present at all times. I had a little kitchen alcove in our classroom that I closed off with chairs. Tell the children that the pot is very hot and they are not allowed to get close.)

5 Keep adding chunks of wax until the liquid wax fills the container up to but no more than three-quarters full.

6 While the wax is melting, set up the area for dipping. Use a table that is the children's height. Cover one end of the table and floor beneath it with newspaper. (Use newspaper for this activity. If you used oil cloth (PVC), it would get covered in wax.)

7 When the wax in one container is all melted, carry it carefully to the table with potholders and place it near the end of the table. Seat yourself by the container and give the children their wicks. Now they begin to dip. Ask the children form a line, holding their wicks. One child at a time comes over to the container to dip. I held their hand and helped them dip their wick down into the wax singing: *"Dip it down; pull it up."* The trick is not to leave the wick in the hot wax for too long. The wax then melts off the wick, instead of building up a new layer.
Straighten the wick for each child after they take it out by gently tugging on the bottom. As the candles thicken, you can also tap them on a piece of grease-proof paper after being dipped. This flattens the bottom so they'll more easily fit in a candleholder. Then the children walk around the table and the room in a large circle (map out a route beforehand) and go back to the end of the line to be in place for another turn to dip. This little walk gives the wax a chance to harden on the wick.

8 As the wax is used up, exchange containers with the fresh batch of melted wax in the water bath. Just add more chips to the old container and return it to the water bath for re-warming. (You want to keep the wax deep enough so the children's candles can be about 10-15 cm tall.)

9 Keep dipping until the children get tired or the candles are about 2.5 cm in diameter, whichever comes first. The youngest children may not make very thick candles, but you can dip them later if you want. The older children may get so involved that they don't want to stop, but don't let the candles get too fat.

10 The finished candles should be approximately 10-12 cm and 2-2.5 cm in diameter. Trim the wicks, wrap them in tissue-paper and tie with a bow, or make a candleholder (see *Wooden candleholders*, page 75) to go with them.

11 Save the pot and containers of hardened wax; you can re-melt them next year.

Rolling candles   *Age 3+*

This is a less time consuming and easier way to make candles. The process is not as magical for the children as dipping, but the candles work, and if you have younger children, these may be more appropriate.

You will need
- wicking (available at craft shops)
- wax sheets (available at craft and art shops — they look like a waffle or honeycomb)
- scissors

What to do

1 Cut the wax sheet into 20 x 10 cm rectangles. Lay the rectangles on the table with the 10 cm side toward you.

2 Place the wicking along the 10 cm edge. Trim the wicking so that it extends 2.5 cm beyond the wax.

3 Begin to roll the wax tightly around the wicking. The younger children may need help getting started.

4 Continue to roll the wax until the entire sheet is rolled. Generally, the more snugly you roll, the better the candle will burn — just don't roll so tightly that you crack the wax.

Decorating candles   *Age 3+*

This is a way to make "shop bought" candles much more personal and beautiful. The decorating wax is very thin and goes a long way, so just give the children tiny bits at a time.

You will need
- candles (white or natural colour work best)
- candle decorating wax (very thin sheets of coloured beeswax). If you can't get special candle decorating wax, you can use regular modelling beeswax. Just use very tiny pieces and warm them in your fingertips until you can stretch them quite thin (see Appendix).
- trays or baskets

What to do

1 Cut the sheets of decorating wax into small pieces (approximately 1.5 x 1.5 cm) and separate by colour. Putting the different colours in individual trays, piles or baskets makes it easier to keep the colours separate while you are working.

2 Let the children take a small piece of wax, warm it in their hands and press it on the candle, smoothing it out and shaping the colour as they go along. You can actually make a picture on the candle with the coloured wax (older children like to do this), or you can simply cover the candle with colours, which is easier for the younger children. Watch that each piece of coloured wax is spread thinly and firmly attached to the candle, not just stuck on. Also, the candle will burn better if the pieces of wax are added side by side, not one on top of the other.

NOTE: A lovely alternative decorating technique uses dried and pressed flowers, fern, grasses, leaves — any flat natural object. After they have been pressed in a flower press or thick book, dip them in melted paraffin or use a small paintbrush to brush the melted wax onto the back side (if there is one) of the objects. Then press them gently and firmly onto the sides of the candle, brushing on more wax if needed. This method works well with large diameter candles rather than tapers.

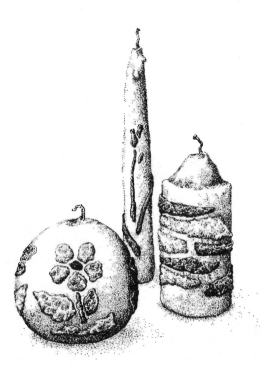

MAKING YOUR OWN VALENTINES

Valentine hearts *Age 3+*

This is fun to do and results in simple but lovely Valentine greetings. Giving children the opportunity to make their own cards, rather than just buying them at a shop, enables them to create rather than consume. Get out the coloured paper, glue and scissors and let them have fun!

You will need
- coloured sugar paper (red, white and pink
- white glue or glue sticks
- children's scissors (don't forget a pair or two for left-handers)
- paper doilies (these aren't too expensive and add a nice touch)
- red felt pen

What to do

1 Show the children how to cut hearts on a fold. Fold the paper, and along the fold draw an "elephant's ear." Cut this out on the fold, and you have a symmetrical heart! Vary the size of the elephant's ear to make larger or smaller hearts. This method is much easier than trying to draw the whole heart.

2 Glue different colour and size hearts on top of each other, on doilies, and so on. Let the children have fun.

3 Sit and cut lots of different size hearts for the little children to use. You can also be the message writer, if need be — perhaps using a red felt tip pen.

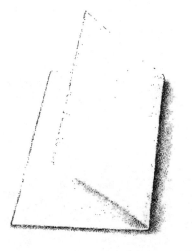

Valentine mice   *Age 3+*

Heart shapes can also turn into mice!

You will need
- red paper hearts
- black felt pen
- bits of string about 8 cm long
- glue

What to do

1 Fold the paper heart in half and find the mouse. The nose and whiskers are at the tapered end — draw them in (see illustration).

2 For the tail, glue the string on the inside of the fold (opposite the end with the nose and whiskers), and let it hang out. There's the mouse!

3 Greetings can be written inside.

Valentine swans   *Age 5+*

A bit more complicated to make, so these are better for older children. They are very lovely.

You will need
- thick white paper or card stock (water-colour paper works well), or use white drawing paper for the swans and mount them on a piece of red sugar paper or card
- pen or pencil
- scissors
- white glue or glue sticks

What to do

1 Fold the paper. Place the swan pattern (see illustration) on the folded edge and trace it onto the paper. Older children may be able to do this.

2 Cut the swan out, helping those children who need it.

3 Open the folded swans. You can write a message inside the folded swan. If you used lightweight paper, glue the swan to red sugar paper or card folded like a card and write the message inside the card.

Growing your own
Valentine　*Age 3+*

These need to be started a week to ten days before you want them to be finished.

You will need
- cellulose sponges (they are much nicer to work with than the synthetic variety. Get pink ones if you can.)
- scissors
- a tray or dish to put the sponges in (they will be damp)
- grass seed (any quick germinating kind)
- mister or spray bottle
- small red sugar paper or card hearts
- glue
- toothpicks
- white paper bowl or jar lid

What to do

1 Cut the sponges (one for each child) into heart shapes about 8-10 cm wide. You don't want them to be too small or too big.

2 Let the children wet the sponges and place them on a tray or saucer.

3 Sprinkle the grass seed over the tops of the sponges, covering the surface.

4 Keep the heart gardens in a sunny window and water each day. The children love to do this, using a mister or spray bottle.

5 The grass should sprout quickly and grow tall and green. Wait until it gets at least 2.5 cm or more tall before finishing the gardens.

6 Add little hearts — one or two per garden. Glue the hearts to the top of the toothpicks and stick the other end into the sponge. Write each child's name on one heart and stick it in his or her sponge the day you make the gardens to keep track of whose is whose.

7 If you are doing this at school, you can send the heart gardens home on Valentine's Day. A heavy weight white paper bowl or a clean jar lid can support the garden on its way home.

NOTE: Another activity for Valentine's Day is to make sachets in the shape of hearts (see *Herbal sachets,* page 76).

3 Spring

The season's garden in spring

For more information on setting up a season's garden, see page 23.

Colours: pastels — pinks, pale yellows, spring greens, violets.

Objects: fresh flowers, small bird nests, dyed eggs (as a symbol of rebirth), polished stones or special rocks, budding branches (in water).

Wreath: Remove the evergreens from your winter wreath. Bind it with wild grasses or weeds, adding flowers here and there for a touch of colour. You could also twine ivy around the straw base, again adding flowers for colour.

Plantings: Just as the children create small dish gardens for a springtime activity (see *Dish gardens,* page 103,) let them help you create a class garden in a large clay plant saucer. If you have had moss in yours for the winter move it to one area of the saucer or transplant it to the outdoors. Now place soil in the saucer, being careful not to disturb any small bulbs you may have planted in autumn. Sink a large sea shell or jar lid down into the soil so that its edges are even with the top of the soil. This can become a small pond when filled with water. Lightly dampen the soil with a plant mister, and let the children help you sow grass seed all over the saucer garden. Remember not to sow the seeds too thickly, but make sure all the soil is covered with seed. Sprinkle with a light "blanket" of soil and thoroughly mist again. Remember to ask the children to mist the seeds, or grass as it grows, each day.

You can add a small blooming branch or flowers and the children can help you create lots of little beeswax characters to live in the garden. A small white duck or green frog can live in the little pond; perhaps a rabbit or deer in the tall grass; maybe a little red dwarf by the rocky mossy area. A robin might build its nest in the budding branch; and there might even be eggs in the nest. The season's garden can become a whole story. The possibilities are endless!

As the grass grows, you can cut it when it gets too long using a pair of scissors. We used to send our fresh grass clippings as a treat for one of the children's pet rabbits, but you could also put them on your window sill for nest-building birds, or at least, put them in your compost heap.

Spring cleaning

The idea of spring cleaning takes on new meaning when trying to make our surroundings more Earth-friendly. Examining the environmental impact of the four basic categories of classroom items becomes essential to spring cleaning. The four categories are cleaning and household supplies; arts and crafts materials; food and drinks; and plastic and paper goods. The issues we need to consider when choosing these items are discussed in the Introduction (see page 16.)

Starting an outdoor garden

Working with the Earth to create a garden, however small, is an experience that every child should have. The rewards for this caring and tending go far beyond the harvest of vegetables, flowers and fruit. As the winter days pass and spring produces new growth, gardening is probably the single most important thing that you can do with children to make them experience this season at its fullest.

A fuller description of setting up an outdoor garden with children is given in the Introduction on page 25.

ACTIVITIES AND CRAFTS

Round wind wands *Age 2+*

These "wind wands" or "round wind catchers" are lovely for those first bright spring days.

You will need
- thin cane (one piece per child, approximately 92 cm long)
- streamers (the crêpe paper variety, approximately 3 cm wide)
- transparent tape
- masking tape

What to do

1 Start with a piece of cane about 92 cm long, and holding both ends together with one hand, twist it around itself, forming a sturdy circle.

2 Bend the twisted cane into a round shape, and thoroughly secure the ends with masking tape.

3 Let the children select five to seven streamers.

4 Attach the streamers side by side by folding a streamer end over the cane and taping it to itself and the cane.

NOTE: These round wands are good for younger children because they can't poke anyone accidentally.

Streamers on a stick   *Age 4+*

A magic wand with frills — these are very appealing to the children and provide lots of possibilities for imaginative play.

You will need
- round sticks or lengths of pole approximately 30-40 cm long
- streamers (the crêpe paper variety work well — cut them to the width desired. The streamers should be approximately 3 cm wide and 60 cm long.)
- transparent tape

What to do

1 Let the children choose the colour streamers for their wand — three to five per wand.

2 Twist the streamers tightly together at one end, and then attach them to one end of the stick with the tape. Make sure that the tape is adhering to the stick and not just to the streamers. By twisting the streamers together and placing them on the top of the stick, the tape has lots of contact with the stick. If you are using natural sticks, wad some tape over the top end to make them less easy to poke with.

3 Depending on the children, you may decide not to allow the wands to be used indoors, as the space may be too confined. Make some rules about the use of wands before you take them outdoors. Make sure the wands have lots of room to move, and tell the children to be careful not to bump or poke others, while they are running.

Blowing bubbles *Age 3+*

Make-your-own bubbles are pleasant to use and much more economical than commercially made bubbles. Keep a litre jar full of bubble mixture handy, and use it to create beautiful rainbow bubbles, inside and outside, whenever appropriate.

You will need
- litre jar
- tablespoon
- mild liquid soap (certainly something non-toxic)
- glycerin (available at chemists)
- straws or bubble wands (you can make these by twisting wire into the desired shape)
- little jars or cups to hold each child's portion of bubble mix

What to do

1 Mix bubble stuff by gently combining a tablespoon of liquid dish soap and a tablespoon of glycerin with a litre of water. Stir them together gently so the mixture isn't too bubbly at this point.

2 Make the rules clear before the children begin to blow bubbles. When we blew bubbles on rainy days, we all sat around a large table. We had the following three rules:

Only pop your own bubbles — not someone else's.

Don't blow into the jar, as this quickly exhausts the bubble stuff.

Stay in your seats — no running around chasing bubbles indoors. Watch them float around the room.

For indoor bubble blowing, these rules helped to create a quiet, calm atmosphere. Outdoors, of course, is different, as the children can chase the bubbles. Just don't run with the bubble stuff.

TIPS ON CONTAINERS: Glass baby food jars with the labels removed (also used for painting) can be washed and re-used. The glass isn't a problem if you are sitting down indoors and things don't get wild. Use them outdoors only if the children aren't walking or running with their containers.

TIPS ON BLOWERS AND ON BLOWING: Straws work well for indoor blowing and are available in large quantities. Be sure that the children dip the straw into the bubble mixture, take it out and blow the bubbles gently into the air. If they blow directly into the jar, the bubble stuff gets too bubbly and is quickly used up. However, since it does make a pretty fountain of bubbles, allow this at the end of bubble time. Tell the children that their bubble stuff won't work if they blow into the jar (too much air gets into the liquid and it won't blow single bubbles.)

Some children need to learn to blow — watch the little ones who may only know how to suck in! Hold their hand by your mouth and blow gently on it. If they still can't do it, sit them near you and blow their bubbles for them. Older children need to learn to blow gently (again, demonstrate on their hand), as blowing too hard pops the bubble just as it comes out. Another discovery the children can make is that if you're sitting at a table, you can blow bubbles on to the table. Dip your straw into the bubble stuff, and while holding it near the table, gently blow the bubbles onto the table top, creating "bubble domes." The children can have a great time making connecting bubble villages and blowing bubbles inside bubbles. For outdoor blowing, bubble wands work better, and you won't have to worry about the children walking or running with straws in their mouths.

Pinwheels   *Age 4+*

Perfect for a breezy day. See what the wind can do! Or the children can create a wind of their own (if nature isn't cooperating) by running or blowing!

You will need
- coloured sugar paper or heavy white watercolour paper that the children decorate with crayons
- pins (the type with coloured round heads, sometimes used on maps or pin boards)
- new unsharpened pencils with rubbers
- scissors

What to do

1 Cut the paper into 18 cm squares. You can vary the size with a larger square, but the pinwheel will be more floppy. Don't get bigger than 21 cm.

2 Determine the centre of the square (see illustration). This is done by lightly folding tip number one to tip number three and tip number four to tip number two. You don't need a strong crease. The centre is where the two folds intersect.

3 Now, using the scissors, cut in on each fold line about three-quarters of the way to the centre. Leave the last 2.5 cm of each fold uncut.

4 With a pin and pencil ready, fold every other tip (you now have eight) into the centre and overlap them. Push the pin through these overlapping tips, through the centre of the pinwheel and into the rubber. Don't let the pin stick out the other side of the rubber.
A little paper washer reinforces the centre of the pinwheel. Cut a small circle of coloured paper (about 2.5-3.5 cm in diameter). This doesn't have to be a perfect circle — just do it freehand. Put a tape loop on the back of the washer and press it onto the overlapping tips of paper at the pinwheel's centre. Then insert the pin. This provides extra support at the stress point.

5 Show the children how to make the pinwheel turn by blowing on it. Then let them take the pinwheels outdoors and see what the wind can do.

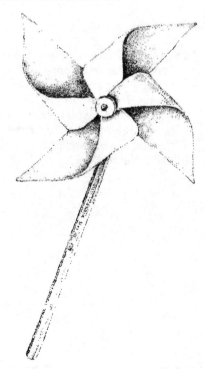

Kites   *Age 3+*

Kites for young children do not need to be the elaborate kind which are totally sky worthy. While these are attractive, and all children should have the experience of flying a kite with an adult, they are often quite happy to make a simple little kite of their own that will flutter up behind them as they run. Then they aren't disappointed if it's not a windy day!

You will need
- heavy coloured paper (sugar paper or watercolour paper, card or posterboard)
- scissors
- crayons
- tissue-paper (cut into streamers approximately 60 cm long by 3 cm wide)
- tape
- heavy string
- sharp pencil

What to do

1 Cut a standard diamond kite shape from paper. It should be approximately 30 cm from top to bottom and 23 cm from side to side. The size can vary, as long as it's not too small. If you trace the form on paper, older children can cut it out by themselves, depending on the thickness of the paper.

2 If you are using white paper, let the children decorate their kites with crayons. Put their name in a corner.

You can also let the children paint their kites with watercolours. (See the description of watercolour painting in *Art and craft materials,* page 16.) Let them paint the paper, then cut the diamond kite shapes when the paper is dry, or cut the paper into kite shapes and let them paint it.

3 Let the children choose three to four streamers and attach them firmly to the bottom corner with tape.

4 Attach a length of string (approximately 90 cm) to the centre of the kite by punching two holes (a sharp pencil will do fine) just to the left and right of the centre and threading the string through the holes. Tie the strings in a knot on the underside of the kite, and then reinforce the holes by placing two or three pieces of tape over them on both front and back. This will keep the string from tearing through the holes when the children are pulling their kites.

5 Once outdoors, let the children run with their kites trailing behind them. It's amazing how much they enjoy these kites with their fluttering streamers.

Dish gardens *Age 3+*

A little saucer can become a beautiful spring garden.

You will need
- small clay saucers, about 10 cm in diameter. These are the kind you put under flower pots — often plant nurseries will sell them at a discount if you buy a large enough quantity. Or use small china bowls or even heavy paperboard bowls. They just need to be low and wide.
- crayons
- potting soil
- grass seed (a quick sprouting variety if possible. You don't need much; ask friends for leftovers.)
- bowls
- spoons
- plant mister or spray bottle
- small sea shells
- beeswax
- tiny branches
- tissue-paper

What to do

1 Write each child's name on the bottom of the saucer with a crayon.

2 Let the children decorate the outside rim of their saucer with crayons.

3 Set up a potting table with bowls of soil, large spoons, a bowl of seed and a plant mister. The children spoon the soil into their dish, filling it about three-quarters full. They often prefer to use their hands for this. Then moisten the soil with the mister, sprinkle on a good layer of seed (not too thick, but make sure to cover the soil surface well) and cover with a thin layer of soil. This last thin layer is not absolutely necessary, but the children like to "tuck the seeds into bed." A final watering with the mister, and the garden can be put in a sunny window to be watched with anticipation for the first signs of life.

Moisture is the key to sprouting. The gardens should be watered once daily (more if they seem to be drying out) — perhaps give them a good drink before you leave for the day. The mister or squirt bottle works well for this as it doesn't flood the seeds and dislodge them. Most of the children will come eagerly to do this task each day.

4 Let the children add a little upside-down shell to the centre of the garden before the grass starts to sprout. This tiny basin will hold water and becomes a little pond in the garden.

5 Once the grass has sprouted, make the gardens a lively place. Use modelling beeswax to embellish the gardens. The children can form all sorts of little things from it: rabbits, birds, baskets of coloured eggs, flowers, and so on. (For a more detailed description of using the beeswax see *Beeswax modelling,* page 86.)

6 Push a tiny spreading branch (the tip of a large branch) into the soil to become a little tree. Glue on tiny balls of pink tissue-paper for blossoms and, perhaps, add a beeswax bird sitting on a beeswax nest. Fill the shell pond with water and add a beeswax duck sitting on the edge. The possible variations for these gardens are as broad as your (and the children's) imagination!

7 A little sprig of forsythia or other blossoms add a nice touch.

Butterfly pop-up cards *Age 4+*

This is a simple idea that can be adapted for any occasion. The pop-up makes it more intriguing. You can make other little pop-up figures depending on the occasion and the interests of the children — birds, rainbows, hearts. Older children can make their own. Adjust the size of the paper figure to the size of your card, and once the older children get the hang of the accordion fold, be prepared for them to want to fold everything in sight!

You will need
- card (card works better but sugar paper will also do. Choose light, springtime colours or ask the children to colour white paper.)
- sugar paper — some cut into little butter-flies (see illustration) and some cut into little strips 2 cm wide by 15-20 cm long
- crayons
- scissors
- white glue or glue sticks

What to do

1 Fold the card in half or in quarters to make the size card you want. The size of the butterfly should also vary with the size of the card. The size butterfly illustrated works with an 21 x 30 cm (A4) sheet of paper folded in quarters (in half top to bottom and in half again side to side).

2 Let the children colour the front (and maybe the back) cover of the card. If you are using sugar paper, be sure to choose lighter colours so the drawing and decorating will show.

3 Give each child a butterfly and a small strip of paper. Show the children how to fold the strip accordion style — front to back, not over and over. This becomes a little paper hinge.

4 Put a small dot of glue on the underside of the butterfly and attach it to the top of the hinge.

5 Glue the bottom of the hinge to the centre of the right-hand side of the inside of the card.

6 When you open the card, the butterfly will gently rise up.

7 Make sure the children's names are on their cards. Write a message if desired, or allow the children to decorate the inside of the card with crayons.

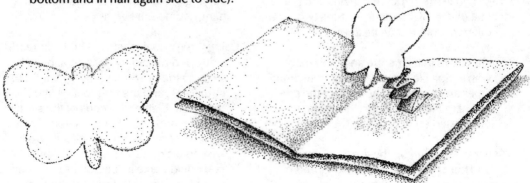

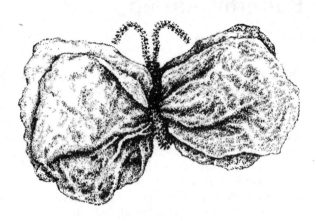

Tissue-paper butterflies and mobiles *Age 4+*

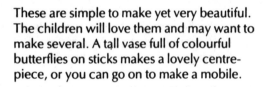

These are simple to make yet very beautiful. The children will love them and may want to make several. A tall vase full of colourful butterflies on sticks makes a lovely centre-piece, or you can go on to make a mobile.

You will need
- coloured tissue-paper cut into rectangles 7.5 x 13 cm, with rounded corners and in light spring colours
- pipe cleaners (white is fine but coloured will do) about 12-15 cm long
- thin string, heavy thread or embroidery floss
- round sticks or lengths of pole
- pieces of cane
- ribbons or crêpe paper

What to do

1 Take two tissue-paper rectangles and place one on top of the other — using two different colours can be attractive.

2 Gather them in the centre and bind them with a pipe cleaner by twisting it several times around itself. The ends of the pipe cleaner will be the butterfly antennae; the twisted section will be the body.

3 Separate and fluff up the tissue-paper wings and bend back the pipe cleaner anten-nae to shape your butterfly.

4 Tie a heavy thread or light string through the top of the butterfly (go under the top of the pipe cleaner). By holding this string and moving their arms around, the children can make the butterflies fly. Or tie the butterfly's string on the end of a stick if you are outdoors. This makes it very special, like a magic wand. Just watch that no one gets hurt and that the children aren't running with the sticks — running is for "stickless" butterflies only.

5 Butterflies attached to small round sticks can be placed like flowers in a vase to make an attractive centrepiece.

6 To make a mobile, bend the cane into a ring (approximately 15-20 cm in dia-meter) and bind it with heavy thread, string or embroidery floss. Then wrap it with colourful ribbon or crêpe paper. Tie the butterflies onto the ring of cane, varying the lengths of string so that they hang at different heights.

7 Using three equal lengths of heavy thread, string or embroidery floss, attach each string to the rim of the ring. Space them equally around the ring so it will be balanced. Gather the ends of the strings together and knot. Hang the mobile over your season's garden. Each child may wish to make his or her own mobile, or you could make a general mobile, made up of individual children's butterflies.

Natural egg dyeing

Age 4+

The egg is really a wonderful springtime symbol of rebirth and the new growth which begins at this time of year. Using spices and vegetable scraps to colour eggs is magical, fun and inexpensive — a bit of alchemy for your children!

You will need
- onion skins from brown onions (the paper-thin, outer brown skins. Ask your grocer if you can clean out the onion bin; usually the skins will be yours for the taking. You will need approximately 300-400 g of skins. These make a beautiful golden brown colour.)
- tumeric (the spice), a heaped tablespoon or two. Tie it up in a bit of cheesecloth to make it less messy and to avoid speckles (although speckles are attractive, too).
- red cabbage (the large outer leaves work best)
- vinegar
- measuring spoons
- white eggs
- large pot(s)
- egg cartons
- rubber bands
- long-handled spoon
- tiny leaves of flowers
- pieces of nylon stocking or cheesecloth
- twist ties

What to do

1 For onion skins and tumeric, boil the material in a pot of water for 30 minutes or so. Then strain and add warm, hard-boiled eggs. You can also boil them in the dye pot instead of in advance, but be aware that some will crack. Add two tablespoons of vinegar when you add the eggs. Simmer the eggs for 10-20 minutes and remove them with a long-handled spoon. Cool them in an egg carton.

2 For red cabbage, wrap the *raw* eggs in cabbage leaves, completely covering the eggs. Hold the whole bundle together with rubber bands. Add two tablespoons of vinegar and the egg bundles to a pot of water and simmer just below boiling for 10-20 minutes. Remove them from the pot and unwrap when cool. This makes lovely blue eggs with a tie dye effect. (NOTE: Raw eggs seem to take the colour better than cooked when using this method.)

3 Resist dyeing — this method works especially well with the onion skins or tumeric. Ask the children to collect tiny leaves or flowers. Press them flat onto the eggshell and hold them in place with pieces of recycled nylon stocking or re-usable cheesecloth. Pull the material tightly around the egg and hold it together at the bottom with a twist tie. Dye as normal, and when you remove the "wrapper," your little leaf or flower will have left its impression.

4 Experiment with other fruits or vegetables. This is not an exact science, so be creative, have fun and expect some unexciting as well as exciting results.

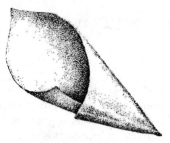

May baskets   *Age 4+*

The old tradition is to celebrate the first of
May and the coming of flower-filled warmer
weather by dancing around a maypole.
Another way to celebrate is by making little
cone-shaped baskets which you quietly, and
in secret, hang on your neighbour's door.
Your little gift will bring great pleasure.
Surprises like this are always nice, and
children love to be the "surprisers."

You will need
- small flowers and greens (clover blossoms,
  dandelions, forget-me-nots, crocuses,
  buttercups, violets, and so on. Keep
  them in water until you're ready to fill
  the baskets.)
- 21 x 30 cm (A4) sheets of white sugar
  paper or watercolour paper
- scissors
- crayons
- clear tape
- tissue-paper and aluminium foil

What to do

1 Fold the 21 x 30 cm paper into four equal
   rectangles by creasing the sheet in half
   side to side and then top to bottom.
   Now cut these out. The rectangles will
   measure about 10.5 x 15 cm. Each of
   these will become a basket.

2 Cut 1 cm wide strips from a 21 x 30 cm
   (A4) sheet of paper. These strips will be
   handles.

3 Let the children colour the baskets and
   handles with crayons, or use coloured
   sugar paper in light spring colours.

4 Shape the rectangles into cones as follows.
   Wrap corner B down and overlap it over
   corner C about 1 cm, keeping the edges
   straight. Tape these two together. Corner

D becomes the bottom of the cone.
Wrap it around to form a point and tape
it in place.

5 Add a 1 cm wide paper handle by taping it
   to the inside top of each cone. Put the
   tape over each end of the handle and
   press it into place inside the cone.

6 Let the children choose a few flowers for
   their baskets. It's good to bind the flower
   bottoms with a bit of wet tissue-paper
   and aluminium foil. The flowers will stay
   fresh longer.

7 Ideally, you could make these the day
   before May Day, and encourage the
   children to hang the baskets quietly on a
   neighbour's door early in the morning. If
   you have made the baskets at school,
   you could either send them home with
   the children, or you could creep quietly
   through the school placing the baskets
   on doorknobs. If you can choose a time
   to do it undetected, all the better.

Flower or leafy crowns   *Age 4+*

These make beautiful springtime costumes. We made extra ones to keep in the classroom. The children wore them out! They are also wonderful for all to wear to a May celebration as you dance around the Maypole. This is another one of those handwork projects that can be kept in a basket and done over a period of days. I required everyone to make one, but they didn't have to work on it every day. Some children will sit down and do the whole thing in a day, others need coaxing to come and reminders to finish. Little ones need lots of assistance which sometimes older, more capable ones can provide. The Leafy Crowns originated one year for the benefit of some older boys (6+) who just couldn't bear the thought of wearing a flower crown. It somehow gave them the opportunity they needed to be different and still allowed them to participate. They wore the leafy crowns to the Maypole celebration.

You will need
- ribbon (choose light spring colours: pink, light green, light blue, pale yellow. The ribbon should be about 2 cm wide and long enough to go around the child's head with two 10-15 cm streamers down the back. I used grosgrain ribbon as it wasn't as slippery as the shiny varieties and was easier to work with.)
- tissue-paper (again choose light spring colours, although I did use a deeper green and a dark greener-blue for Leafy Crowns. Cut the tissue-paper into rectangles 5 cm wide by 13 cm long and sort according to colour.)
- needles and thread (knot a doubled thread to avoid unthreading)

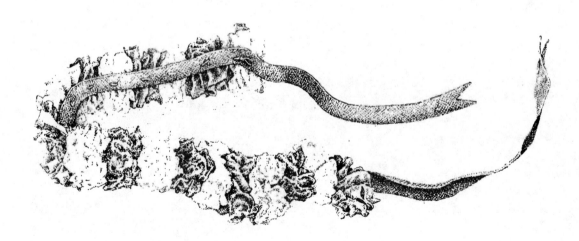

What to do

1 Give each child a ribbon cut to fit his or her head (don't forget to add another 20-30 cm for streamers). Also, give each child a needle knotted and double threaded with about 30 cm of thread.

2 Ask each child to choose a rectangle of coloured paper and sew a running stitch lengthwise down the centre of it, scrunching it as they go. Then gather this "blossom" or "leaf" by pushing the tissue-paper down to the end of the thread. The blossom is then tacked onto the ribbon by sewing down through the blossom and the ribbon, and then up through the ribbon again so the needle ends up on the top of the ribbon, ready to stitch another tissue-paper blossom.

Remember to begin attaching blossoms about 18 cm from where the crown will be tied to allow for knotting and for the streamer. Also, fluff and/or scrunch the tissue-paper to make it more "blossomy."

3 Continue to gather and stitch these blossoms onto the ribbon until you reach a point 18 cm in from the other end. After stitching on the last blossom, knot off the thread on the back of the ribbon. The closer the blossoms, the more beautiful the crown will be. Choose a random selection of colours, or encourage the children to set up a pattern and stick to it, for example: pink, green, yellow; pink, green, yellow or dark blue, dark green; dark blue, dark green. The children enjoy this sequencing, anticipating what will come next.

4 When the ribbon is full of blossoms, except for the knot and the streamer allowance at each end, tie it around the maker's head and marvel at what a beautiful thing they've created!

Pressed flower
cards   *Age 4+*

This project needs to be started a couple of weeks before you want to finish it so that the flowers have time to dry. The cards make lovely Mother's Day greetings (see also *Butterfly pop-up cards,* page 105).

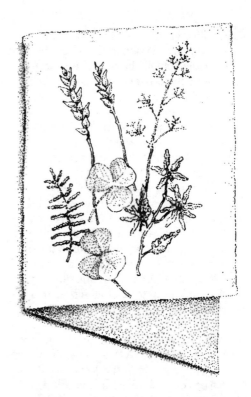

You will need
- a flower press or heavy book, such as a telephone book
- some absorbent paper, such as plain newsprint or sugar paper
- attractive paper for the cards — sugar paper (in pretty spring colours: green, yellow, pink, or light blue) or water-colour paper
- glue sticks, or white glue, small dishes and cotton swabs
- wax paper
- crayons
- coloured pencils

What to do

1 A couple of weeks before you want to make the cards, gather flowers, grasses, weeds and so on, to dry. You can dry anything, even weeds look lovely. Keep in mind that the thicker the item, the less likely it will dry well. For example, a dandelion is too fat to dry well, although you can certainly try one as an experiment.

2 Begin pressing the flowers and so on, before they wilt, so bring the flower press (or telephone book) outdoors, or bring the items indoors fairly soon after you've picked them. Arrange them on the blotter sheets of the press or between the folded sheets of absorbent paper if you are using a heavy book. The pressed flowers dry the way they are placed in the press, so take time to straighten them out and spread the flower petals. Older children love to help with this. Also, place each item separately on the paper — do not overlap them. If using the telephone book, do not use pages next to each other. It is better to leave chunks of pages between each place with flowers.

3 Tighten the fastening screws or belts of the press, or place something heavy on top of the telephone book — another telephone book will do.

4 Carefully check the drying items after several days. When they are ready to use they will actually be dry. Then carefully remove the flowers and store them flat — perhaps between sheets of paper — until you are ready to use them. You can then add other items to dry. Change the absorbent paper when needed.

Drying things from nature is something you can do year round, starting with colourful leaves and autumn flowers, winter grasses and hardy weeds, and springtime buttercups and clover leaves. The technique is the same, the children love to do it, and you can build up an accumulation of items to be used for cards, tables, posters or bulletin board decorations or to put in the season's garden.

5 Make cards by folding a sheet of paper in half. 21 x 30 cm (A4) works well, but use any size you like (just don't make it too big or you will use up all the dried flowers very quickly.)

6 On the front of the card, the children arrange a few of the dried items, then glue them down. Glue sticks are less messy to use, but a dish of white glue with cotton swabs (and reminders to use just a little!) will work. Apply the glue lightly to the paper and gently press the flowers onto it.

7 Lay the card between a folded sheet of wax paper so it won't stick, and put it in or under a heavy book for 30 minutes or so to give the glue time to dry.

8 The children can draw a picture inside the card. You can write a short message for the children, using coloured pencils rather than magic marker pens. They have a softer, lighter touch.

Flower necklace
or lei   *Age 4+*

These are beautiful and can be made with
any number of different flowers; experiment
and be creative. Hyacinths make a particularly lovely, sturdy, sweet smelling version.
They are excellent Mother's Day gifts and
very attractive to wear when dancing around
the Maypole.

You will need
- fresh flower blossoms (one good-sized
  hyacinth will make one lei. Other blossoms may be used, just look for those
  that are small and sturdy, something that
  can be strung easily and will lay nicely.
  Scented blossoms are particularly attractive.)
- needles
- thread (start with about 60 cm for each
  child)
- tape and pen

What to do

1 Gather flowers. If you are at school, you
  could ask each child to bring one
  hyacinth from home, or you could get
  them from the florist. They are usually
  available cut or potted in flower shops in
  early spring. You want nice, tall, full
  blooming ones. The red and white
  varieties seem to hold up better than the
  purple which get slimy and soft a bit
  more quickly, but all kinds will work. If
  you tell the florist what you are doing
  and that you want to buy a large
  quantity, perhaps he or she will give you
  a discount. (Hyacinths are wonderful
  bulbs to plant in the garden, along with
  narcissus and daffodils, to be enjoyed in
  the spring.)

2 Gently remove the blossoms one by one from the stems. If the children are helping with this, make sure they grasp each blossom at its base and gently wiggle or twist it off. You don't want them to be torn or bruised. Do this just before the stringing.

3 Double thread your needles and tie a knot about 10 cm in from the end. This will give you room to tie the two ends of the necklace together when you have finished stringing.

4 Thread the blossom onto the string, by pushing the needle up through the bottom centre of each blossom. Slide the blossom gently down to the knotted end. Continue threading until you have about 10 cm left on the thread. Make single colour necklaces or experiment with multi-coloured ones.

5 Tie the two ends of thread together to make the necklace. It's attractive if it is a continuous circlet of flowers, but it's okay if there is empty space on the back or on the sides. Put a piece of tape on each necklace and mark it with the child's name. Keep the necklaces refrigerated if you are not using them right away. They will stay beautiful for a day or two, depending on the type of flower used, but don't expect much more than that.

NOTE: If you make the thread for each necklace long enough so that it will slip over a child's head easily, it won't have to be untied. Slip it on over child's head as you thread her or his needle to assure a proper fit. If the children are making them for their mother or another adult, make them a bit bigger.

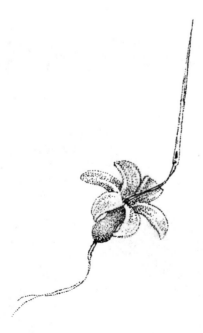

Making butter   *Age 3+*

Children love to eat butter. It's a wonderful moment when they experience that their efforts have transformed the cream into butter. A trip to a farm to get the cream would really complete the picture.

You will need
- heavy whipping cream (one that is not ultra-pasteurized works much more easily. Try a natural food shop.)
- two or three clean marbles
- a clean, clear container with a tight fitting lid
- spatula
- plate
- wooden spoon
- clover or parsley (optional)

What to do

1 Pour the cream into the container and add the clean marbles. Put the lid on the container, and be sure it is closed tightly.

2 Begin to shake the contents up and down and side to side. Keep shaking until the cream turns into butter. It will get lumpy and the whey (a watery, milky liquid) will separate out. The time required for the butter to come varies depending on the temperature, the kind of cream used and other factors. Just keep at it and be patient. The children enjoy shaking the container and listening to the sound of the rattling marbles get more and more muffled as the butter thickens. Chant or sing (make up a very simple tune) the following verse while doing the shaking:

> Come, butter, come,
> Come, butter, come.
> Mary's at the garden gate,
> Waiting with a butter plate.
> Come, butter, come,
> Come, butter, come.

(Substitute the name of the child who is shaking.)

This rhyme can also be used as a way to measure the length of the shaker's turn, particularly if you have a lot of children waiting to take a turn. Go through the verse twice for each turn.

3 When you have butter, scrape it out of the container with a spatula and put in on a plate. Then "paddle" the butter; this means pat it all around with the flat back of a wooden spoon or other utensil to shape it into a little butter cake and to paddle out any whey.

4 Decorate the little butter cake with tiny blossoms or green leaves, for example, clover or parsley. Some people press "butter stamps" onto the cake which leave decorative impressions.

5 Use the butter with bread — preferably some you have baked — or crackers for a snack or at meal times. Home-made butter is a special treat for a festival meal.

NOTE: We set up a little butter churning station with two chairs at the end of a table and the materials. The children could come and help as they wished. I would sit in one chair and the "shaker" was in the other. A clean glass jar (labels removed) is easy to see through, and the top won't come off with all the shaking. Choose a jar that is small enough to fit into the children's hands comfortably, yet large enough to let the marbles really rattle around and agitate the cream. If you use glass, be extra careful and wipe the outside of the jar periodically so it doesn't get slippery.

WOOL

Washing wool *Age 3+*

A field trip to the farm to watch a sheep being sheared is a wonderful spring experience. Have a picnic lunch there, and bring back some of the newly sheared wool. Then begin happy days working with wool. If you take the children to a farm to see a sheep sheared, be sure to speak to the farmer first about how it will be done and how the sheep feel about it, so you will be ready to reassure the children. The job is often done with electric shearers, and sometimes the sheep are nicked and bleed a little. They aren't always so cooperative at "haircut" time. A wonderful story to tell or read to the children when you begin working with wool is *Pelle's New Suit* by Elsa Beskow (see *Useful reading,* page 154,) which tells the entire story of a new wool suit, starting with the lamb.

You will need
- some raw fleece (if you can make a trip to a farm to get some, great. Otherwise, try weaving or wool shops. Just be sure to get "raw" fleece that has not yet been cleaned or carded. Wool batting or stuffing has already passed this point.)
- two full wash tubs (one with a very mild pure soap and one with clear rinsing water)
- drying rack or clothes line
- basket

What to do

1 Pick through the fleece to remove large bits of field débris, sticks, burrs and so on. The children are often amazed at how many things stick to the sheep's coat.

2 Tear off handfuls of the fleece, squish them in the soapy water, then rinse them in the rinsing water. This is fun to do outdoors during outside play time. If you do the washing outside, then you don't have to worry about wet floors and spills. It's also interesting to note how oily the wool feels. This is the natural lanolin in the wool — it gives the wool its characteristic "sheepy" smell. Leave some of this lanolin in the wool, as it makes it easier to work with.

3 Spread the little clumps of wool to dry on the clothes line or drying rack.

4 When the wool fleece feels thoroughly dry, which will depend on the size of the clumps, whether you spread them out a bit to dry and the weather conditions, gather it into a large basket.

5 The wool is now ready for the next step, carding.

Carding wool   *Age 4+*

The actual purpose of carding wool is to get all the fibres of the wool going in the same direction so it can more easily be spun into wool. It's a pleasant activity to do — indoors or out — and the children love the little fluffy clouds of wool that result.

You will need
● wool carder (it's nice to have a pair of real ones for the adult to use, but they are often a bit large for the children to use comfortably. I have had great success using small wire-toothed brushes which pet shops sell for brushing animals. They are not too expensive, so you may want to buy several pairs, as children will want to help. The brushes will last for years.)
● basket of washed, raw wool
● second basket

What to do

1 Set up a carding circle — a chair for you and several small chairs and sets of carders for the children around a basket of washed wool. A second basket holds the carded wool when it's ready.

2 Take a small bit of wool — you will gradually be able to gauge how much to take — and stretch it over the outside edge of one carder. Then show the children how to "brush" that wool with their other carder — always moving in the same direction, not going back and forth. The carder holding the wool does not move, the other one does. The children brush each bit of wool until there are no clumps and it becomes a fluffy little cloud of wool. You will see

that if you put too much wool on the teeth of the carders, you will not be able to brush through it. If you put too little on, it almost disappears as you card it.

3 Place the carded wool into the second basket. This is an activity which can go on for weeks. In fact, I often keep wool for carding available. It's just the thing for children who need some sitting down or who can't decide what to do.

4 You can also card the wool — though not as thoroughly — by teasing and spreading out the little lumps with your fingers. This will sometimes satisfy little fingers until they have a turn with the carders.

NOTE: It is not necessary to have a lecture-demonstration lesson with little children. They come and go and truly enjoy the work going on in their presence. It gives them such a sense of satisfaction, as if they were doing it themselves, and they will learn all they need to know by being there and by seeing firsthand the process by which a sheep's wool begins to become something to wear.

Spinning wool   *Age 4+*

You can actually spin wool with your own hands! But if you are lucky enough to know how to spin or can invite a spinner into your classroom, the children will benefit by seeing the wool actually become wool. Drop spindles are not so hard to use — I taught myself by following the directions from a book and practising a bit before trying it in front of the children.

You will need
- drop spindle (check in a weaver's shop or a wool shop)
- spinning wheel (you might be able to go and visit a spinner, or if you are working in a school get someone to come and spin in the classroom. The children love to see a spinner at work.)

What to do

1 You can actually "spin" wool into wool by rubbing little carded handfuls of it back and forth in the palms of your hands. You might not be able to knit a sweater with the results, but the children will get the idea.

2 Drop spindles are not difficult to use. This is not something for the children to do, rather they can watch it being done, and know that people invented tools, such as the drop spindle and the spinning wheel, to help them work more effectively. They needed wool to make their clothes, blankets, and so on.

3 Contact a weaver's shop or perhaps a wool or craft shop to learn about someone who spins wool. Go and visit a spinner, or if you are in a school invite a spinner into your classroom, and the children will not only see the carding being done but also what comes next. It's as if they were seeing straw spun into gold! Ask the spinner to set up and work during free play time, and all the children will gather round.

Weaving with wool

Age 5+

Weaving is a more complicated activity and as such is appropriate for the older children, but it is also wonderful for younger children just to watch and experience the process.

You will need
- a cleft branch — with a V-shaped fork that is not too wide — for a loom. (Gather a number of these over time, perhaps during walks in the woods.)
- heavy thread or string.
- wool (from a wool shop or specialist supplier, but ideally wool that you have spun yourself)
- scissors
- feathers, stems of grass, brightly coloured wool (optional)

What to do

1 String the warp thread onto the branch loom by tying it to the left side of the branch near the bottom of the "V." (The warp is the threads that form the basis for the weaving.)

2 Bring the thread (or string) over to the right branch, wrap it tightly all the way around the branch several times, then go back and around the left branch. Continue doing this back and forth wrapping until the base of the "V" is completely strung, leaving 3-5 cm at the end of each branch unstrung. This "margin" will keep the weaving from slipping off the ends of the branch.

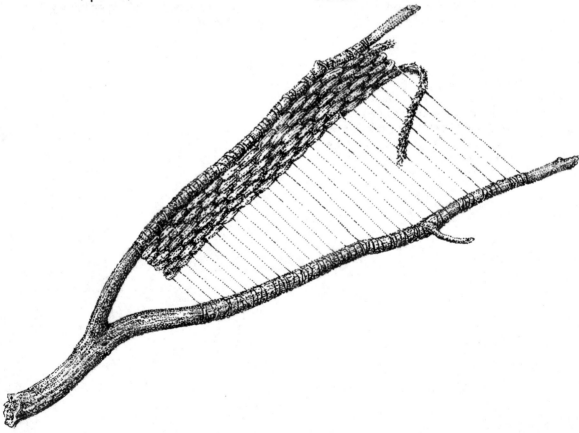

3 Begin weaving with the wool, going alternately over and under the warp threads. You may either cut the wool to the length you need to weave one strand from the bottom to the top of the warp, or you may use whatever length wool you have and weave continuously, wrapping around the topmost warp thread and weaving back down, always alternating over and under the warp threads. When you come to the end of your wool, tuck the end in, take a new strand, overlap it a bit over the strand you just finished weaving, and continue from where you left off. Try alternating or changing colours. If you weave with the individual strands of wool, tuck the ends in for a more finished look.

More simple weaving can be done by using unspun wool. Just take a handful of the wool and roll and form it loosely into a "log" shape. Weave with this, adding new wool as necessary. Using this "fatter" unspun wool is easier for little fingers.

4 As you are weaving, be sure to press the vertical strands of wool close together. The more closely you press them the tighter your weave will be.

5 Weave until you reach the right-hand side of the branch and the loom is full. Weave in a feather, a long stem of grass or a bit of brightly coloured wool as a decoration. Use your imagination.

6 If you have woven fairly tightly, you can cut the weaving off the loom by carefully snipping the warp threads and tying the warp ends together. (This is why you wrapped the warp ends several times around — to leave enough for knotting.) The weaving will also look beautiful as a wall hanging just as it is, especially if you add some decorative elements as mentioned above.

4 Summer

The season's garden in summer

For more information on creating a season's garden, see page 23.

Colours: bright blues, greens, reds, yellows, pinks.

Special objects: shells, sea objects, flowers or weeds that are going to seed, summer produce of all kinds, such as a bowl or basket of strawberries, cherries or tomatoes, and so on.

NOTE: Food placed in the season's garden should not remain there indefinitely. It can be placed there one day and brought to the children's attention, perhaps with a short story about where it came from or how it grew. But it should be enjoyed for a snack or used in a cooking project before it has a chance to spoil.

Wreath: Your wreath can really become a flower wreath in the summertime. Using a base of straw, wild grasses or weeds, you can bind on all kinds of flowers, wild or culti-vated. Many flowers actually continue to look quite beautiful even after they've dried and faded, so you don't have to replace them constantly. It's also nice to add some little bumble bees, as these are familiar summer visitors. Shape them from yellow wool or beeswax, adding a bit of dark colour for contrast (even dark blue or purple will do as black is not always available), and using string, hang them from the wreath.

Plantings: It's fun to turn your dish garden into a tiny beach for summer, and it gives you a chance to remove the soil, moss, grass or whatever else you've cultivated during the year so that you can start afresh in the autumn. The moss, bulbs or plants can be replanted outdoors in appropriate spots or, if necessary, put in the compost heap. Add the soil to the compost as well. Fill your contain-er about half to three-quarters full with sand. You can add a shell or small saucer of water, too, if you like. Then place different kinds of sea shells, special stones and other sea objects in the sand. Pieces of beach glass (smooth, weathered bits of broken glass you often find washed up on the beach) are often fascinating to the touch. The children will love to come and sift the sand through their fingers and play with the shells.

The outdoor play area

Summer gives us the chance to look carefully at the outdoor spaces where our children play. An outdoor play area is a space that can easily be taken for granted, but it offers many opportunities for enhancing an aware-ness of nature and for creating interesting spaces for both work and free play. Ideas for creating a more "natural" outdoor play area are given in the Introduction on page 22.

ACTIVITIES AND CRAFTS

Shooting star streamer balls *Age 5+*

This sewing project is a bit difficult, but the results are a wonderful summer toy. You may want to just make a few for your class to play with outdoors. If you are very industrious and/or have access to a sewing machine, they make great leaving-for-summer gifts for the children.

You will need
- sturdy fabric (solid colours are best, red cotton knit or red wool felt are especially nice)
- needles and thread
- rice or sand for filling
- ribbons (two to three per ball — each approximately 50 cm long in hot colours: red, orange, yellow, gold)

What to do

1 Cut the fabric into 8 cm circles. You will need two circles for each ball.

2 On a machine or by hand using a small, sturdy stitch such as a backstitch, sew the circles together about 1 cm in from the edges, leaving an opening for filling. Older children will be able to sew this by themselves, but younger children or those less experienced in sewing will need assistance.

3 Overlap the streamers and pin them to the inside of this opening. Stitch them firmly in place.

4 Turn the entire ball "inside out" (you have been working on the inside) so that all the stitching is now on the inside and the outside is out!

5 Fill with rice or sand (not too full), fold in the edges and stitch up the opening. It is important to stitch this carefully so the shooting star doesn't leak!

6 Let the children take them outside and throw them up into the air or back and forth to each other. The ribbons will stream behind the shooting star as it flies.

NOTE: While some children may not be able to do the stitching required for these, as it needs to be small and close together so the filling won't leak out, they love to choose their ribbon colours and do the filling. A nice idea is to make them for an end-of-year or summer festival. Invite other parents, then each parent can make one with his or her child. It helps to have the circles sewn together and the ribbons pre-cut. Then let them take it from there.

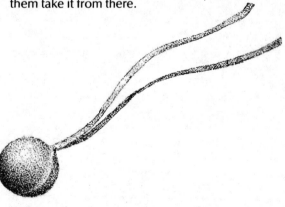

Butterfly crowns   *Age 3+*

These unusual crowns also make beautiful window pictures. The children can wear their crowns for an outdoor summer festival — a part of which might be acting out the poem included below.

You will need
- sugar paper (any colour except black or brown)
- transparent sticky-backed paper or tracing paper with wax paper and glue
- hole punch
- wool or ribbon for crown ties (cut in pieces approximately 30 cm long)
- scraps of tissue-paper (light colours)
- stapler

What to do

1 Fold a 21 x 30 cm (A4) piece of sugar paper in half from top to bottom and cut the butterfly shape on the fold.

2 Cut out the centre of the wings on both sides (see dotted lines) to make the frame.

3 Cut transparent sticky-backed paper to cover the hole in the wing frame and attach it to the back. Now you have a butterfly with a sticky space for a wing!

4 Prepare the crown headbands by folding a 21 x 30 cm (A4) piece of sugar paper lengthwise to make a 2-3 cm band. Fold

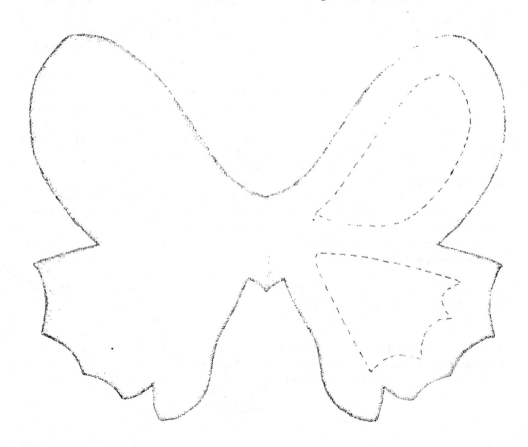

this band over two or three times to make it sturdy. Crease the folds well. Use a hole punch to make holes about 3 cm in from each end of the band. Tie a piece of wool or ribbon through the holes.

5 Give the children the butterfly shapes and scraps of coloured tissue-paper. They tear off small pieces of the tissue-paper and stick them to the paper frame of the wing. Encourage them to fill the wing space completely; overlapping tissue-paper pieces is fine. (NOTE: You can also pre-cut or tear the tissue-paper if you like. Tearing is nice as it gives the tissue-paper a soft edge. Just be sure that the children tear off small pieces of tissue to stick onto the frame.)

6 Staple the bottom of the finished butterfly to the middle of the headband. Make sure to match the colour of the head-band to the butterfly frame, so a yellow headband goes with a yellow butterfly, and so on. Mixing the colours of the frames is distracting and makes the finished project less beautiful.

7 The following poem holds lots of possibilities for play:

A tired caterpillar went to sleep one day,
In a snug little house of silk and grey.
He said as he softly crawled into his nest:
"Ah, crawling is fine, but rest is best."
He slept through the winter long and cold
All tightly up in a blanket rolled.
'Til at last he awoke on a warm, spring day
To find that winter had gone away.
He awoke to find he had golden wings
And no longer need crawl over sticks and things.
"Ah, crawling is fine," said the glad butterfly
But the sky is best when you learn to fly.

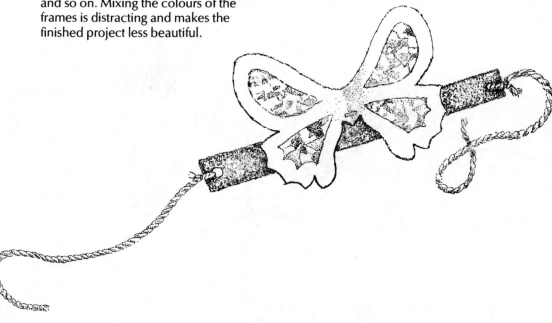

Dandelion chains   *Age 4+*

This can be done indoors, but is really more appropriate when the children are playing outside. You can substitute other flowers, such as daisies, though dandelions are readily available — they even grow through cracks in the pavement! Beside being beautiful crowns, the chains make lovely decorations for your season's table or castle decorations in the sandpit. The children love to watch you make something from "nothing."

You will need
● dandelions or other flowers with tubular stems

What to do

1 Gather dandelions. Children love to do this — just show them how to pick them so you get a nice long stem.

2 Use your fingernail to make a small slit (1-2 cm) in the dandelion stem about 3 cm below the head of the flower.

3 Slip the next dandelion through the slit, stem end first, and pull it through until it stops at the flower head.

4 Continue making slits and attaching dandelions until the chain is the length you want. To make a crown, attach the last stem to the beginning of the chain. You can twine it around the first flower or knot it to the stems.

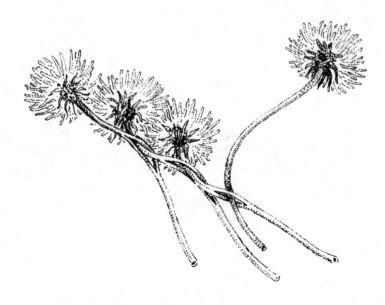

Walnut boats   *Age 3+*

These are very easy to make and can be used indoors, outdoors in a tub or water table or in the river if you are lucky enough to have one nearby!

You will need
- walnut shells (you want perfect half shells, so crack them carefully)
- small bits of beeswax or clay (beeswax works better as it doesn't dry out)
- string cut in 23-30 cm lengths
- paper scraps
- scissors
- toothpicks
- buttons (optional)

What to do

1 Crack the nuts and let the children help you remove them from the shell. This may mean snack time to them! Save the rest for a baking project. (NOTE: A friend tells me that an oyster shucker is great for opening walnuts when you don't want to break the shells. Just stick it in the little opening often found at the flat end of the walnut and wriggle it open.)

2 Place one end of the string in the bottom of an empty walnut shell and press a small ball of beeswax over it to hold it in place.

3 Cut a tiny sail shape from the scraps of paper and run the toothpick through it. Now the boat has a sail on its mast.

4 Stick the bottom end of the toothpick into the ball of beeswax.

5 If you want, attach a button to the loose end of the string. This gives the children more to hold on to as they pull their sailing boats around the water.

Creating mossy islands (water play)   *Age 3+*

Creating this play area is fun and easy, and once created, it becomes a little world in which children can spend countless happy hours of play. If you can bring it outdoors, that's even better.

You will need
- large container to hold water (sand or water table, galvanized tub, basins)
- large and medium-sized rocks
- moss (collect a bit from where it grows naturally: moist areas in the woods, stream banks, and so on. Dig it up carefully with a layer of dirt and keep it moist in transport. Repair the area from which you removed the moss by filling holes and patting down loose soil, and don't take too much from any one place.)
- walnut boats from the previous activity, or corks, toothpicks and paper
- beeswax, sticks and string (optional)

What to do

1 Arrange the rocks in the centre and corners of the water container, building them up to make little cliffs or mountains. (Create caves by leaving spaces between the rocks.) Make a little beach near the bottom of the cliff by putting some sand on top of a flat rock. If you are using a small basin, you may want only one "island" in the middle.

2 Carefully add the moss to the rocky islands making them green and lively. Make sure the moss has a good foundation of soil, adding some if necessary. Pat and fit the moss into the rocky spaces. You don't need to cover the rocks entirely. These are the mossy islands, and depending on the amount of moss you have been able to collect, you may want to have only one mossy island and leave the others rocky.

3 Fill the container about half full with water. You want enough water to make it fun to play in without flooding the islands and beaches.

4 Allow the children to play in the water with the walnut boats. You can add little beeswax people who live in the rocky caves and visit the beaches. Corks (usually available in bags of assorted sizes at the hardware store) with toothpick and paper sails also make nice boats, buoys or channel markers. The children can gather small sticks that can be lashed together to make docks or rafts.

5 Keep the moss moist by misting it daily. When the islands are finished with, the moss can go into your season's garden, or patch damp areas of your playground, or it can be returned to its natural home.

Bark boats   *Age 4+*

A very simple little boat with a leaf sail.

You will need
- chunks of bark in varying sizes from about 10 cm long to as big as you can handle. Pine bark (mulch) is available at garden centres.
- sticks
- leaves
- some kind of tool to bore a hole with, such as a hand-operated drill, an oyster shucker, awl or ice pick
- small cup hooks and string (optional)

What to do

1 Bore a small hole in the centre of the piece of bark to hold the mast for the sail. If you have a very large piece of bark, you may want to have more than one mast. Show the children how to bore the holes. They will need a variable amount of supervision depending on the sharpness of the tools they're using.

2 Thread a large leaf onto a stick, and place the stick in the hole.

3 If you want to attach strings so the children can pull their boats (or not lose them downstream!), screw a small cup hook into the front edge and tie on a string.

4 Sail the boats in a big tub of water or water table or, better yet, take the children to a river or stream and really let them sail!

Parachute people   *Age 3+*

A fun and easy way to explore the air. Take these to the top of the climbing structure and see what happens.

You will need
- 20 x 20 cm squares of lightweight cloth, such as muslin. (Cheesecloth will also work as long as the weave isn't too loose and open. You can also use recycled paper, tissues or napkins.)
- thread
- beeswax or plasticine

What to do

1 Tie the thread to the four corners of the cloth by scrunching up each corner, wrapping one end of the thread around it a few times and tying a knot. Leave the other end of the string free.

2 Attach the other three strings. Gather the string ends together and tie them into a knot.

3 Embed the knot string in a ball of beeswax or plasticine, and if you like, form a little person. Just make a very general shape; don't make it too detailed.

4 The older children will be able to make these on their own. The younger ones may need some help or may just want to play with them.

Paper birds   *Age 4+*

The air is full of birds in the summertime. These little birds with folded paper wings can hang from a string or be attached to the end of a stick. The children love to "fly" them.

You will need
- sugar paper (red, yellow, blue, white)
- scissors
- drawing paper or tissue-paper (white or coloured)
- crayons
- string

What to do

1 Cut the sugar paper into bird shapes. Use the shapes illustrated or invent your own.

2 Cut a small slit in the body where the wings should be.

3 To make the wings, cut a small rectangle from the drawing or tissue-paper. If using drawing paper, you can let the children colour the "wings." Fold the rectangle accordion style (back and forth) and slide the folded piece through the slit in the body. It should be a tight fit.

4 Spread the folded wings a bit. You can also glue the top edges of the two wings together so that they stay open. Attach a piece of string to the body at the top of the back.

5 Let the children "fly" the birds by holding the string or tying it to the end of a stick. Just take care that the sticks are used carefully.

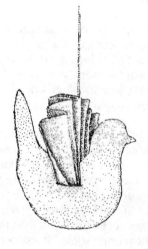

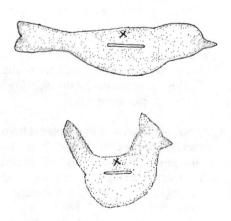

Moving pictures   *Age 4 +*

Children love pictures that move, as the movement makes things come alive. Your oldest children will enjoy making these themselves; the younger ones can help you make some for the class to use.

You will need
- heavy drawing paper (at least 21 x 30 cm, about A4 size)
- crayons
- scissors
- tape
- support sticks (lollipop or craft sticks, tongue depressors or strips of smooth cardboard)
- glue (optional)

What to do

1 Ask the children to draw and colour a simple sea scene on the paper. Basically you want to include the sea, the sky, some fish, sea birds, and so on. Don't just make line drawings, but fill in the area with colour.

2 Cut a slightly curving line through the middle of the paper, making sure to leave a 3 cm margin on each side of the paper. Place a piece of tape at each end of this curving cut on the back of the paper. This will reinforce the paper. Also be sure to cut it no higher than the length of your support sticks. The stick needs to reach the cut and still be longer than the bottom edge of the paper.

3 With the children's help, draw a small sailing boat on a separate sheet of paper. Heavy paper, such as watercolour paper, works well for this. The boat should be a size that will fit in with the scene — not so big or so small as to seem out of place.

4 Cut out the boat and glue or tape it to one end of the support stick. The boat should be wide enough to cover the width of the support stick, so the support stick does not show.

5 Slip the stick through the hole and down past the bottom of the paper. Set the boat into the slot so that it appears to be part of the scene.

6 You can add extra support to the scene by gluing the same size piece of paper to the top and two sides of the back of the scene. Leave the bottom open for inserting the stick.

7 Sail the boat along the sea, perhaps stopping to swim or to look for a whale! Endless adventures can develop from such a simple starting place.

8 As you can imagine, this simple technique can be adapted for many different kinds of scenes. You could have a little child on a stick walking in the woods or up a mountain, or an animal wandering through a meadow. Experiment with new possibilities. The more difficult ones may be too hard for the children to do, but they will love to watch and help you make them for the classroom and to play with them when they're done.

BUILDING PLAYHOUSES OUTDOORS

The bean wigwam *Age 3+*

Children love to build their own houses, and summer is the perfect time to move this satisfying out-of-doors activity. If you don't have long branches and sticks in your garden or playground, hunt elsewhere for them, or buy canes at your local garden centre. Your efforts will be well rewarded. This house will not only provide a place to play, it will provide food as well!

You will need
- garden spade or fork
- sticks, branches, garden cane or bamboo (at least 2 metres long)
- string or strong twine
- runner bean seeds (any kind will do although the scarlet runner bean variety has the added advantage of producing beautiful flowers which attract butterflies.)

What to do

1 Prepare the area where you will plant the seeds. If you are planting them in the vegetable garden, plant them near the outside edge, so the children can have easy access to their house without trampling the lettuces! Also, as they are tall when grown, you may want to place them so that they do not stand in the way of the sunlight reaching other parts of the garden. You can also dig up separate areas where you'd like the wigwams to be. Using a spade or fork, turn the earth in a circle large enough to accommodate two or three seated children (about one metre in diameter). Remove any grass or weeds (shaking off the dirt) and place them on the compost heap. Smooth the soil, adding in some compost if you have it. If you don't have a vegetable plot, you will need large low planting boxes or containers, about five of them, spaced in a circle with an opening on one side which will eventually become the door.

2 Place the sticks or canes in the ground around the edge of the circle, leaving an opening on one side for the entrance. You need to use at least five canes to allow for thicker foliage cover. Tie the tops of the branches together in the centre, wigwam-style. Bind them fairly well so they will hold.

3 Plant two to three bean seeds around the outside base of each cane and water well. Keep the earth around the seeds moist and they will sprout more quickly. The watering is an excellent activity for the children.

4 Once the seeds begin to sprout and grow, the plants will reach out with delicate tendrils and climb up the canes.

5 The wigwam house will grow larger and more private as the plants grow. Use your judgment as to when it can be "moved into."

6 The flowers will set into beans. Get the children to help pick the beans when they are fully grown. Top and tail them, cook them in salted boiling water for about three minutes (taking your usual safety precautions if cooking with young children) and they will contribute to a delicious meal.

The stick house   *Age 3+*

This house is fun to make and can provide hours of industrious play.

You will need
- long branches or poles (at least five)
- string or strong twine
- small branches, twigs
- grasses, vines

What to do

1 Help the children set up the long poles that will be the base of the house. Locate them by a wall, in a corner, against a fence or by a tree. Lean them up against whatever support you choose and wrap the tops together with twine. Tie them together tightly at the tops or weave the twine in and out and around, allowing the pole to spread out a bit. This method works if the pole or branches are supported by a fence. You can also, at this point, lash them to whatever support you are using — the fork of a tree, top of a fence, and so on — to make the house extra sturdy.

2 Weave smaller branches, twigs, bits of vine, grasses — really anything — in and out of the long poles from the bottom up. Don't forget to leave a space for the door, and you can also leave holes for the windows. Just stop weaving when you come to the window space and wrap your weaving material around the last pole or weave it back the other way.

3 Weave in these smaller materials until you reach the top of the house. You can always go back and fill in the holes — actually mud works very well for this!

4 The children can do most of the house building. You will just need to get them started by helping them with long poles, or perhaps only by providing the pile of materials and suggesting a house. Show them how to start the weaving, provide occasional help and consultation as necessary and let them do it!

The cloth house   *Age 3+*

We've probably all made houses of cloth, using old sheets, at some point in our lives. Have a basketful of old sheets or covers just for use outdoors and dip back into your childhood memories to get the children started.

You will need
- a basket of cloths or covers of all sizes
- string, twine or rope
- clothes pegs

What to do

1 Take the baskets of cloths outdoors one day and begin to make a roof.

2 Help string up twine where needed to provide places to hang the cloths. Bushes, trees, fences and so on, can all be foundations.

3 Provide technical assistance as necessary!

4 Unlike the bean wigwam and stick house, cloth houses are rebuilt each day. Ask the children to help you fold up the cloths when it's time to go inside. When the cloths need washing, bring water tubs, soap and scrubbing boards out-doors, string up a clothes line and have a wash day!

BERRIES

Berry picking   *Age 4+*

This is the time of the year to enjoy picking, eating and preserving all kinds of berries. The children often love to eat fruit and it is wonderful for them to experience where it comes from.

You will need
- a place to pick berries: raspberries, strawberries, gooseberries, blackberries (later in the year)
- containers
- masking tape and pen
- parents to accompany you

What to do

1 Make arrangements to visit a farm which has "pick-your-own" berries of some kind, going through any necessary procedures for obtaining permission from parents or school. Ask the farm if you need to bring your own containers. If you do, parents will usually help in providing something suitable. You will need one to two for each picker. Also ask the approximate cost for a kilo of berries so that you are prepared beforehand.

2 Prepare the children for their trip by telling them a story about how the trip will go. Be sure to include all the important details like how they will behave in the cars or bus, what kind of clothes they will wear (work clothes: sturdy shoes, long trousers, sun hats and old shirts as berry stains don't come out easily), what they will do when they get there (stay close to you and any other adults, and, of course, never wander off), what the berries they pick will look like (e.g., strawberries will be deep red not orange or white), and how they will be careful not to eat too many or they might get a tummy ache!

3 When you arrive at the farm and receive your instructions for picking, be sure to show the children what a nice, ripe berry looks like so that they will pick good ones. Perhaps each child can pick two containers — one for home and one for the group, but don't count on it.

4 Give each child one container at a time to fill. Have ready a large shallow box (sometimes the farm will provide these, if not bring your own) to hold the filled berry containers. Mark the containers with the child's name using masking tape and a pen, especially the one container they will be taking home. Marking the containers can be done before you set off to save time and aggravation!

5 Pick lots — occasionally cautioning the children not to eat too many although you certainly should expect them to eat some.

6 Don't stack the berry containers on top of each other for the trip home. Otherwise you end up with lots of squashed berries and lots of sad children.

7 Refrigerate the berries that aren't going to be used straight away.

NOTE: Decide ahead of time what you will do in the case of rain. If the farm will let you and the children wear rain gear including boots, go anyway! If it is *really* wet, cancel and choose another day.

Berry shortcake *Age 3+*

Once you've picked the berries, it's good to use some of them to make a special snack the next school day. Berry shortcake is a tasty way to enjoy the fruits of your labour. Let the children help with all the preparation, mixing, and so on.

You will need
- aprons
- mixing bowls and spoons
- measuring utensils
- cake tin (a 23 cm round or 20 x 28 cm rectangle)
- 180 ml oil, plus some for oiling the pan
- 125-180 ml honey, plus a little extra
- 310 ml yogurt or milk
- 2 tablespoons vanilla
- 250 g whole wheat pastry flour
- 1 tablespoon baking soda
- ¾ teaspoon salt
- whipped cream (optional)

What to do

1 Preheat oven to 180°C, 350°F, Gas Mark 4.

2 Mix the wet ingredients — 180 ml oil, 125-180 ml honey, 310 ml yogurt or milk, 2 tablespoons vanilla — in a bowl.

3 Mix the dry ingredients — 250 g flour, 1 tablespoon baking soda, ¾ teaspoon salt — in a separate bowl.

4 Combine the wet and dry ingredients.

5 Pour the batter into an oiled 23 cm round or 20 x 28 cm rectangular cake tin.

6 Bake for approximately 45 minutes, until the top springs back when touched gently with your finger.

7 While the cake is baking, let the children help you rinse and slice the berries (or use them whole) and toss them with a bit of honey. When the cake is cool, spread the berries on the top of the cake, garnish with whipped cream and enjoy it!

Berry cobbler   *Age 3+*

And try some berry cobbler, too!

You will need
- aprons
- mixing bowls and spoons
- measuring utensils
- 20 x 20 cm baking tray
- saucepan and heat source, or an electric frying pan
- 200 g whole wheat flour, plus 1 tablespoon
- 3 teaspoons baking powder
- ½ teaspoon salt
- 35 g butter, plus extra for greasing the pan
- 1 egg
- 125 ml milk
- 1 tablespoon honey or syrup, plus 125 ml
- 300 g berries

What to do

1 Preheat oven to 220°C, 425°F, Gas Mark 7.

2 In a large bowl, mix together 200 g flour, 3 teaspoons baking powder and ½ teaspoon salt.

3 Cut in the butter until the mixture resembles coarse crumbs.

4 In a separate bowl, beat together the egg, milk and 1 tablespoon honey or syrup.

5 Add the liquid all at once to the flour mixture and stir until just moistened.

6 Combine the berries, 125 ml honey or syrup and one tablespoon flour in a saucepan and heat.

7 Bring to the boil, turn down and stir until thickened a bit. Watch carefully so that it doesn't stick and burn.

8 Place berries in the bottom of a greased 20 x 20 cm tray.

9 Spoon the biscuit dough over the top.

10 Bake in a 220°C, 425°F, Gas Mark 7 oven for approximately ½ hour.

11 Let it cool, then enjoy eating it!

Smoothies   *Age 3+*

A very refreshing way to enjoy your berry harvest. Smoothies are a delicious and nourishing snack drink. Once you've learned to make them, you can vary the ingredients endlessly and try new fruit combinations.

You will need
- a blender
- smoothie ingredients (use organic ingredients whenever possible: apple juice, yogurt, honey, rinsed berries. Bananas are optional, but they add taste and thickness.)
- cups

What to do

1 Use apple juice as the base. Place two cups in the blender.

2 Add 125 ml plain yogurt, one heaped tablespoon of honey, 100 g of rinsed berries and one ripe banana.

3 Blend until smooth.

4 Taste a bit and adjust the ingredients, more honey to add sweetness, more yogurt for a more tart taste, more berries for a fruitier taste, more juice to "stretch" the smoothie so there will be enough to go around.

5 Pour into cups and drink for a snack or at meal time.

NOTE: In hot weather, you can add a couple of ice cubes to make it really chilled.

Preserves   *Age 4+*

Making berry preserves from your remaining harvest is not as hard as you might think, especially if you can keep the jam refrigerated until you are ready to use it. You just need a safe place to cook it for a while and you'll be rewarded with delightful fruity smells.

You will need
- colander or strainer
- large heavy pot (large enough to hold the amount of berries you're cooking)
- potato masher
- long-handled wooden mixing spoon
- berries
- spoons
- clean glass jars with tight fitting lids
- sweetener (preferably honey or syrup, but you can use ordinary sugar)

What to do

1 Gently rinse the berries.

2 Place them in the pot and mash them a bit with the potato masher.

3 Begin to cook them, stirring frequently, until the mixture is simmering all over the top). Then turn it down to medium-low.

4 Stir in the sweetener half a cup at a time, tasting (with a clean spoon) for sweetness. If the berries were very sweet, you won't need as much. Remember, the jam doesn't have to be as sweet as "shop bought." It's good to taste the berries.
  I usually use natural unrefined sweeteners such as honey, maple syrup, or syrup when cooking or baking as they contain vitamins and minerals and as such are healthier than processed, refined sugar. However, they are more expensive and in a situation where you want to use a fair amount — as in making jam — you can substitute sugar with the understanding — which you can convey to the children — that jam, like other sugary things, should be eaten only occasionally.

5 Stir carefully and frequently during the cooking process so the jam doesn't stick and burn.

6 When it has cooked down and thickened a good bit, turn it off and let it cool. It will continue to thicken as it cools.

7 Spoon into clean glass jars and keep refrigerated until you are ready to use it.

Freezing berries   *Age 4+*

Freezing berries is kind of the opposite of making jam, using cold instead of heat to preserve the fruit. But it is an easy way to save the whole berries for future use, and all you need is a freezer. Younger children can certainly help with this, just expect as much eating as helping!

You will need
- colander or strainer
- berries
- clean towels
- baking trays
- freezer space
- plastic containers with tight fitting lids (re-use those yogurt containers used for the smoothies, page 143)
- adhesive freezer labels

What to do

1 Rinse the berries carefully and lay them out on clean towels to drain.

2 Place them on the baking trays side by side — keep each berry separate so cool air can circulate around each berry. Put them in the freezer overnight.

3 The next day remove them from the baking tray and place them in a plastic container. Use adhesive labels to mark the date and the kind of berry. Just like frozen grapes, frozen berries make a very cooling and healthy summer snack.

NOTE: This is an easy way to preserve almost any fruit you want to save. You can even save peach slices if you first toss them with a bit of lemon juice to prevent darkening. The frozen fruits make a wonderful garnish for a birthday cake or add a special touch of summer to a fruit salad.

Basket weaving   *Age 5+*

This activity is one is a good challenge for the older children. But it is also wonderful for the younger children to watch and experience the adults around them doing "real" work — work which results in things that they can see and use. It is especially nice to work on the basket outdoors. The children will be very interested in what you're doing and will probably ask you if they can help.

You will need
- weaving materials (you can try almost anything which feels flexible and sturdy enough to weave: willow wands, vines, Virginia creeper, wild grapes, honey-suckle, ivy, and so on. Vines work well because you can get long continuous pieces to weave. You can also use "shop bought" cane for weaving, or use cane for the base and natural materials for the weaving.)
- brown paper bag

What to do

1 Gather your weaving materials, strip off the leaves (the children love to help with this), coil them loosely and place them in brown paper grocery bags to "cure" for a few days. The curing can be omitted if you are pressed for time, but it helps make a better basket.

2 Select the thickest material or "shop bought" cane. From these make two rings approximately 18-20 cm in diameter. The size of the rings will determine the size of your basket, so don't make them too big or too small. 18-20 cm in diameter is a good size for a first effort.

3 Place the two rings together at right angles to each other. Lash them together at the intersecting points using the "God's Eye" wrap. (Wrap around each post from behind and go to the next and wrap around, and so on.) This makes the frame of the basket.

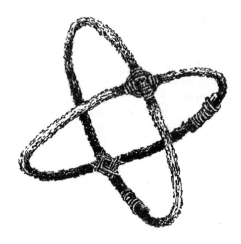

4 Now make the warp. Wrap the bottom of the basket with weaving material by running them from side to side to form the warp on the bottom of the basket. Wrap around the top edge, go down and over or under the bottom seam, and up around the opposite edge. They don't need to be tight together. In fact, you can space them 1-2 cm apart because you need room to weave between them. Continue until the bottom of the basket is full.

5 Now comes the real weaving. Take weaving material, and starting on the sides near a God's Eye, begin to weave over and under the warp pieces. Overlap loose ends (these can be tucked in later) and continue weaving until the basket is complete. The more tightly you weave, the sturdier the basket.

6 If the children want to help, let them do some of the over and under weaving, helping them as needed.

7 Use the finished basket to hold toys or supplies or to carry flowers or green beans in from the garden. It is wonderful for the children to experience the making of something from, apparently, nothing.

Appendix

Sources for materials
(Contact information for suppliers is given on p.151)

Beeswax and beeswax sheets
Fred Aldous Ltd
Candle Makers Supplies
Helios Fountain
Specialist Crafts Ltd.

Beeswax crayons
Helios Fountain

Candle making
Fred Aldous Ltd
Candle Makers Supplies
Helios Fountain
Specialist Crafts Ltd.

Cane
The Cane Store

Cleaning products
Earth-friendly cleaning products are now available in most supermarkets. The Ecover brand is popular.

Composters
Aerobic composters (the sort which need a constant flow of air from below) are available from the Centre for Alternative Technology.

Dyeing
For further information on supplies for natural dyeing, see the following:
Natural Dyes and Home Dyeing, Rita J. Adrosko, Dover Publications Inc, 1971.
The Complete Guide to Natural Dyeing, Eva Lambert, Search Press Ltd, 2010.
Colours from Nature: A Dyer's Handbook, Jenny Dean, Search Press Ltd, 2009.

Felt
Fred Aldous Ltd
Helios Fountain
Most craft shops and fabric shops or market stalls sell felt in large quantities but you may have to check that it has a high wool content.

Fleece
The British Wool Marketing Board
The Rare Breeds Survival Trust

Food Mill
Manual food mills (often referred to as "moulis") can still be found in kitchen shops. Manual coffee grinders work just as well for the activities in this book, and can be found in kitchen shops, including Boots.

Mulching products and organic manures
Garden Organic
Garden Direct

Natural watercolours
There are an increasing number of watercolours available which are "natural" to a greater or lesser extent. Most are on sale in artist's or craft shops.

Recycled paper
This is widely available in stationers and craft shops. It can also be bought online from a variety of sources, including Recycled Paper Suppliers.

Stuffing
The most Earth-friendly material for stuffing is kapok, available from haberdashers or most large department stores. Various types of stuffing can be ordered from Bear Basics.

Tissue paper
This is widely available from stationers and craft shops, including Fred Aldous Ltd.

Vegetable and herb seeds
Untreated vegetable and herb seeds are available from Garden Organic and the Centre for Alternative Technology.

Wool
Natural wool and weaving yarn is available from British Wool.com.

Wreath frames
A variety of frames are available at most florists. You can buy an oasis frame — dry for dried wheat and flowers, wet for fresh flowers. Or you can buy the empty wire construction for a moss frame. You can then gather moss with children and secure it to the frame by winding another length of flexible wire backwards and forwards around the two concentric circles of the frame. Wreath frames are also available through the Craft Depot.

Addresses of suppliers

Fred Aldous Ltd
www.fredaldous.co.uk
+44 (0)161 236 4224

Bear Basics
www.bearbasics.co.uk
+44 (0)1963 34500

British Wool
www.britishwool.com

British Wool Marketing Board
www.britishwool.org.uk
+44 (0)1274 688666

Candle Makers Supplies
www.candlemakers.co.uk
+44 (0)207 602 4031

The Cane Store
www.canestore.co.uk
+44 (0)1975 651386

Centre for Alternative Technology
www.cat.org.uk
+44 (0)1654 705950

The Craft Depot
www.craftdepot.co.uk
+44 (0)1458 273569

Ecover
www.ecover.com
+44 (0)8451 302 230

Garden Direct
www.gardendirect.co.uk
+44 (0)845 217 0788

Garden Organic
www.gardenorganic.co.uk
+44 (0) 24 7630 3517

Helios Fountain
www.helios-fountain.co.uk
+44 (0)131 229 7884

Rare breeds survival trust
www.rbst.org.uk
+44 (0)24 7669 6551

Recycled Paper Suppliers
www.rps.gn.apc.org
+44 (0)1676 533832

Specialist crafts Ltd
www.specialistcrafts.co.uk
+44 (0)116 2697711

Traidcraft
www.traidcraft.co.uk
+44 (0)191 491 0591

Other Useful Addresses

British Glass Manufacturers Confederation
www.britglass.org.uk
+44 (0)114 290 1850

British Plastics Federation
www.bpf.co.uk
+44 (0)20 7457 5000

Friends of the Earth
www.foe.co.uk
+44 (0)20 7490 1555

Greenpeace
www.greenpeace.org.uk
+44 (0)20 7865 8100

Oxfam
www.oxfam.org.uk
UK: 0300 200 1300
Overseas: +44 (0) 1865 47 2602

The Nature Conservancy
www.nature.org
+1 (800) 628-6860

Soil Association
www.soilassociation.org
+44 (0)117 914 2406

Waste Watch
www.wastewatch.org.uk
+44 (0)20 7549 0300

World Wide Fund for Nature
www.wwf.org.uk
+44 (0)1483 426444

Useful reading

Adolphi, Sybille, *Making Flower Children*, Floris Books, Edinburgh, 2008.

Barz, Brigitte, *Festivals with Children*, Floris Books, Edinburgh, 1987.

Berger, Petra, *Feltcraft*, Floris Books, Edinburgh, 2010.

Berger, Thomas, *The Christmas Craft Book*, Floris Books, Edinburgh, 1990.

—, *Crafts through the Year*, Floris Books, Edinburgh, 2000.

—, *The Gnome Craft Book*, Floris Books, Edinburgh, 2010.

Blue Peter, *Planetwatch: A Young Person's Guide to Protecting our World*, Dorling Kindersley, London, 2009.

Bom, P. & Huber, M., *Baby's First Year*, Floris Books, Edinburgh, 2008.

—, *The Toddler Years*, Floris Books, Edinburgh, 2009.

Brooks, Felicity & Khanduri, Kamini, *Protecting Our World: A Beginner's Guide to Conservation*, Usborne, London, 1991.

Bryer, Estelle & Nicol, Janni, *Celebrating Christmas Together*, Hawthorn Press, Stroud.

—, *Christmas Stories Together*, Hawthorn Press, Stroud.

Carey, D. & J. Large, *Festivals, Family and Food*, Hawthorn Press, Stroud.

Cooper, S., C. Fynes-Clinton & M. Rowling, *The Children's Year*, Hawthorn Press, Stroud.

Druitt, A., Fynes-Clinton, C. & Rowling, M., *All Year Round*, Hawthorn Press, Stroud.

Earthworks Group, *Fifty Simple Things Kids can do to Save the Earth,* Warner Books, London, 1990.

Hailes, Julia, *The New Green Consumer Guide*, Simon & Schuster, London, 2007.

Fitzjohn, S., Weston, M. & Large, J., *Festivals Together*, Hawthorn Press, Stroud.

Glöckler, Michaela & Goebel, Wolfgang, *Guide to Child Health*, Floris Books, Edinburgh, 2007.

Guéret, Fréderique, *Magical Window Stars*, Floris Books, Edinburgh, 2010.

Henley, Claire, *My First Nature Activity Book,* Scholastic Children's Books.

Jaffke, Freya, *Toymaking with Children*, Floris Books, Edinburgh, 2010.

Kraul, Walter, *Earth, Water, Fire and Air*, Floris Books, Edinburgh, 2010.

Kutch, Irmgard & Walden, Brigitte, *Autumn Nature Activities for Children*, Floris Books, Edinburgh, 2005.

—, *Spring Nature Activities for Children*, Floris Books, Edinburgh, 2006.

—, *Summer Nature Activities for Children*, Floris Books, Edinburgh, 2007.

—, *Winter Nature Activities for Children*, Floris Books, Edinburgh, 2006.

Kutik, Christiane, *Stress-free Parenting in 12 Steps*, Floris Books, Edinburgh, 2010.

Leeuwen, M. van & Moeskops, J., *The Nature Corner*, Floris Books, Edinburgh, 2008.

Litvinoff, Miles, *Earthscan Action Handbook*, Earthscan, London, 1990.

Marion, Isabel, *Christmas in the Family*, Floris Books, Edinburgh, 2006.

Meyerbröker, Helga, *Rose Windows and how to Make them*, Floris Books, Edinburgh, 1994.

Müller, Brunhild, *Painting with Children*, Floris Books, Edinburgh, 2002.

National Geographic Society, *Green Guide Families: A Complete Reference Guide for Eco-Friendly Parents*, 2010.

Neuschütz, Karin, *Sewing Dolls*, Floris Books, Edinburgh, 2009.

Reinckens, Sunnhild, *Making Dolls*, Floris Books, Edinburgh, 2003.

Robbins, Robin, *Your Environment through the Seasons,* Charles Letts & Co, 1991.

Santer, Ivor, *Green Fingers and Muddy Boots: A Year in the Garden for Children and Families*, Floris Books, Edinburgh, 2009.

Schmidt, Dagmar & Jaffke, Freya, *Magic Wool*, Floris Books, Edinburgh, 2000.

Sealey, Maricristin, *Kinder Dolls*, Hawthorn Press, Stroud.

Thomas, Anne & Peter, *The Big Summer Activity Book*, Floris Books, Edinburgh, 2006.

Index